QUICK & EASY
slipcovers

QUICK & EASY
slipcovers

GAIL ABBOTT and CATE BURREN
Photography by Mark Scott

CICO BOOKS
LONDON NEW YORK

Published in 2008 by CICO Books
an imprint of Ryland Peters & Small
519 Broadway, 5th Floor, New York, NY 10012
www.cicobooks.co.uk
First published in 2005 as *So Simple Slipcovers*

10 9 8 7 6 5 4 3 2

A CIP catalog record for this book is available
from the Library of Congress

ISBN-13: 978 1 906094 59 1
ISBN-10: 1 906094 59 4

Printed in China

Project editor: Gillian Haslam
Copy editor: Jane Bolsover
Designer: Roger Daniels
Photographer: Mark Scott
Step-by-step photography: Alicia Clark and Rachel Whiting

Contents

Introduction

You may enjoy searching flea markets and thrift shops for old pieces of furniture that have gone unnoticed. It's amazing how often you can unearth a dated chair or a battered old ottoman that makes its reappearance later, looking smart and stylish with a new slipcover. Give it a tailored, floor-length slipcover, and a worn slipper chair can be transformed into a comfortable, pretty perch for a bedroom. A scruffy footstool, given a good cleaning and a neat slipcover, can become a useful accessory in a dressing room or bath.

You may have a set of hand-me-down dining chairs that you don't want to give away because they belonged to your grandmother. Re-style them with fashionable toile de Jouy fabric. If you're on a budget, but would like to change the look of a dated or soiled sofa, an attractive throw will cover it completely. You'll find a project for any piece of furniture that needs a different look.

If you are new to sewing, you'll appreciate the easy projects that will help you get started. Hem a square of bright checked cotton, for example, and you have a cover for a table; weight the corners and you can use it outdoors, even on breezy days. Learn how to make the easiest pillow cover—no zipper, ties, or buttons required—and you can run up a set in a day to give your bedroom or living room instant new style. If you don't want to sew a stitch, take a look at our instant makeover ideas and make a zigzag shelf cover, an updated version of the old antimacassar to throw over the back of a chair, a lace-up chair cover, or simply tie a square of fabric over a tiny ottoman.

Opposite This antique bench, with storage drawers and basketwork sides, was found in a sale room. With a new set of seat covers, it now takes pride of place in the sitting room. See page 94 for instructions.

6

Above Making your own bed linen gives you the option to design a bedroom exactly as you want it. See pages 122 and 126 for instructions.

Maybe you have more experience with a sewing machine. In that case there are plenty of projects here that will have you making slipcovers for all of your favorite pieces. The armchair cover featured on pages 46–53 is the biggest project in this book, and takes a bit of time to complete. Make a muslin pattern following the step-by-step pictures before you cut any expensive fabric. Don't forget: you can create a slipcover for a sofa using exactly the same methods.

Whatever your skills, you'll find inspiration in these projects, in addition to all the help you'll need, contained within the instructions and their accompanying photographs. Hopefully you'll have fun and enjoy choosing fabrics and getting just the look you want for your home.

Above Cover an old sofa with a printed patchwork fabric for a cheerful family room. See page 52 for instructions.

Opposite In an updated version of a traditional print, a bright floral cover has been slipped over a garden chair to bring a splash of color to a summer lawn. See page 44 for instructions.

INSPIRATIONS

Getting Started

One of the most amazing things is the way that a tired living room can be transformed quickly and easily by the simple trick of covering the sofa with a large throw. Pile the sofa high with a variety of coordinating pillows, and the room will take on a different ambience. In a bedroom, a couple of large square pillows and a throw will add an instant new look without the help of a paintbrush. A round tablecloth draped over a fiberboard table, or a remnant of bright, dotted fabric tied over an ottoman in a playroom are changes that cost very little and are so easy to make. These simple changes are minor miracles. You'll be amazed at how learning to make your own slipcovers will give you the power to make major transformations in every room.

What's Your Style?

Understanding your own personal style is the key to choosing fabrics and colors. Look around your house carefully and ask yourself the simple question—"What do I love?" A home can so easily become cluttered with furniture and items that sneak in unnoticed, so it's a good idea to try to look at each room with a fresh eye every so often. What things you can live without? Get off to a great start by clearing out unnecessary things. If you find yourself hesitating, remember this design motto: less is more. Once you have cleared the decks, you will be left with furniture and objects that tell a very distinct story about your personal style. Is there a particular painting that relaxes you and refreshes your spirit? Or do you have a beautiful mirror

or ceramic bowl that makes you happy? You can use all of these things as starting points for a new design, and to help you make discriminating choices from the bewildering array of fabrics available.

Different Looks

Your home is a reflection of yourself, so following your style will help you to feel relaxed and comfortable in it. It's no good surrounding yourself with flowery fabrics and fringe if your ideal home is an airy beach house with fresh, seaside colors and stripes. If you are a comfort junkie, and

Below Sensual style—a mix of sensuously tactile fabric pillows turn a classically styled sofa into a boudoir. Coordinated textures and colors, tassels, and velvet ribbons give a collection of different pillows a sense of cohesion when grouped together.

love to cuddle up with a soft blanket on a huge sofa, don't get sidetracked by contemporary, minimalist furniture. It's a matter of looking at your lifestyle and fitting your home around your family and the way you live, not some ideal that you've seen in a showroom.

Take into consideration the architectural style of your home, too. On some level you have chosen your environment, so working with it will help create a cohesive living space that will emanate a sense of well-being to everyone who visits. But don't be too rigid about it. Simplicity of line and color can emphasize the details in a room with decorative moldings, whereas a boxy, newly built house can be gain character and warmth with antiques or vintage painted furniture. Making a folder of style ideas will help put you on the right track, so look through home magazines and tear out pictures that appeal. You'll find that you instinctively pick out rooms that are right for you.

Sensuous

Sophistication is the keyword for this look. Choose fabrics with a sheen that reflects the light, in soft, retro shades of crushed raspberry, mocha, and pale creamy tones. Pick out vintage velvet and old lace to make into pillows that soothe the senses, and find scraps of antique fabrics that can be appliquéd for a luxurious look. Sensuous living means comfort, too. Surround yourself with soft textures such as velvet and mohair throws to wrap around yourself. Allow your toes to sink into deep pile carpets and choose feather trims and beaded edgings.

Right Traditional style—a botanical design covers the sofa, with colors drawn from it at the windows and in the pillows. The accessories are plain, but have subtle styling details, such as the buttons and fringe on the pillows, that add texture to the theme.

Traditional

A different kind of comfort, the security of coming home, is symbolized by traditional style. Big sofas that welcome you are covered in floral fabrics in muted tones. Beds may be inspired by the past when draperies were used to close out drafts. Choose your basic fabric and pick out colors from it when making pillows, and accessorize the room with framed flower prints, paintings, and traditional style lamps. Blend a mix of solids and prints, but keep the overall theme serene and peaceful.

Right Traditional style—mixed with plenty of white, a floral dust ruffle and matching canopy still manage to look simple and unassuming, while dark wood furniture gives the room a feeling of stability and tradition.

Tailored

The clean lines of this style will fit in perfectly with a contemporary room. Let the colors be warm or neutral, and choose plain fabrics in crisp cottons and linens. Introduce texture too, using loose-weave fabrics, or add texture in the form of pleated pillows, and keep shapes neat and tailored. Base your design on neutrals and earth tones, and accessorize with pillows and throws in a contrasting hue, adding splash with an accent color.

Contemporary Country

Give any house a simple, airy feeling when you style it with a contemporary country look. This means adding pure white to a pretty floral print, so that the flowers are a charming accessory, not the overwhelming abundance of pattern we have come to associate with the country look. Instead of something fussy and old fashioned, you create an upbeat, modern look that's young and chic. This is a style guaranteed to bring the freshness of the country to town.

Beach House

Bring the beach into your home with bright and breezy stripes and the colors of the sea. This is a look for summer that's perfect for a seaside home, and refreshing in the city, as well. Choose strong white canvas and striped cottons, accessorize with model boats and shells, and line walls with painted bead board. Update ottomans and armchairs with crisp tailored slipcovers, and choose stripes and checks in blue, green, and aquamarine shades. Use

Right Contemporary country style—a dining room is given a modern twist with a white linen tablecloth and upholstered chairs covered in floral slipcovers. The white walls, floor, and paintwork are softened by the beaded chandelier.

Above Tailored style—olive green velvet has been used for the headboard and pleated dust ruffle, while a combination of pure white and taupe bed linen add freshness and color.

Right Tailored style—opt for unassuming checks on a neutral sofa for a clean look to make the most of a modern house.

the beach-house look in a boy's bedroom, a bathroom, or a sunroom.

Ideas

Some of your most beloved pieces of furniture may be old or worn, but you don't want to live without them. Do you have a chair that you always fall into at the end of a hard day? Perhaps it has a deep seat and low arms that mold themselves around you and welcome you home. If the fabric is shabby and faded and comes from another era in your decorating life, keep your old treasure and give it a new look with a slipcover.

A new sofa is expensive, so buy one that is covered in muslin and make a slipcover to protect it. You will be able to relax, safe in the knowledge that no matter what grubby marks appear, your cover can be cleaned easily. We sometimes suggest two sets of slipcovers: one that's cozy for winter, and another that's light and casual for summer.

There's a real thrill to shopping in thrift shops, auctions, and flea markets, too, when you know you can make a slipcover that will totally transform a bargain. Many of the chairs and ottomans used in our projects have been rescued from the back

of a dusty shop, or found at a garage sale. Use pillows randomly and lavishly, but make them in different sizes and shapes. Mix coordinating fabrics together, but don't overdo it—stick to two or three different fabrics and add edgings for extra texture.

Fabrics

A classic chair or sofa can look completely different depending on the fabric you choose to cover it. Pick a crisp striped linen in blue and white with a pleated skirt to cover a sofa, and you have the makings of beach-house style. But cover the same sofa in a traditional floral fabric and your room immediately assumes a traditional feeling. For a romantic look, cover a bedroom chair in a fine sheer fabric, which will look almost translucent in the light. Start with the style you want and pare down your options before you choose a fabric. If you can, get a few fabric swatches and put them together with paint and wallpaper samples to see whether they work together in the room.

Different qualities of light can affect the way a color looks, so a neutral linen that looked beige in the store can look gray when you get it home. If you are planning to cover a three-piece suite of matching sofa and two chairs, a contemporary option is to change the fabrics so that each piece looks different. Cover one chair in a muted floral and the other in a coordinating check, for example, then pick out a solid color from these to cover the sofa.

With the small amount of fabric needed to make a pillow, you might find you can afford to splurge. Use half a yard of luxurious fabric, such as velvet, suede, or

Left Beach house style—a sunroom has been given a clean, blue-and-white look that has all the freshness of the seashore. Narrow stripes cover the chairs and ottoman, and are echoed in the wide stripes of the shade.

Above Find an antique sheet with hand-embroidery, choose a modern equivalent like this one, or sit down quietly and embroider one of your own.

Above A pile of pillows needs to look informal and comfortable, not rigid and stiffly arranged, so make them in lots of different shapes and sizes.

silk, and a less-costly cotton for the back of the pillow. If you are lucky to come across a hand-embroidered or monogrammed sheet, make it into an heirloom pillow that can be seen and appreciated every day.

Practicalities

The best fabrics to use for slipcovers in a family home are tightly woven cottons and linens. Steer away from loose, handwoven fabrics that will pull when exposed to children and pets.

Make life easy for yourself by covering seating in white or natural, washable cotton canvas. It may sound like an anomaly, but you will be able to wash out spills and stains, as well as allergens from dust and animals, time after time. Slipcovers don't have to be washable necessarily, but you will want to have

Left Slip a wisp of gathered organza over a wood chair and a bedroom immediately becomes a romantic boudoir.

them dry-cleaned. So make sure that that the fabric is practical for this use before you buy it.

Cording adds a tailored and professional finish to slipcovers. Use it to strengthen seams around arms and corners, where there is more strain on the fabric. For a less formal look, dispense with cording altogether, and make a cover that has a loose fit and can be pulled on and off easily.

If you are replacing the pillows, don't be tempted to choose cheap foam. There are many grades of foam. Always buy the best you can afford. High-density white foam with a channeled-down wrap is best for seats. Back cushions should be a blend of 75 percent feathers to 25 percent down.

Trimmings

Add glamour and style to a room with any one of the gorgeous trimmings that are readily available in fabric shops. We've given you the basic techniques for making pillows and throws, but there's really no limit to the choice of edgings that can turn a simple pillow into a work of art. Add beads, feathers, braiding, or fringing, and layer patterns for a richly coordinated look. Give a sofa throw an extra dimension, too, with a sumptuous tassel at each corner and a silk edging all around. If you are decorating with a sensuous theme in mind, velvet ribbon and embroidered braiding will add texture; a traditional design will be enhanced with lush, fringed pillows.

Above right This extravagant bead-and-braid trim adds a touch of glamour to a floral pillow.

Left Insert cording into all of the seams of a tailored chair slipcover to strengthen them, especially around the arms and corners of seat cushions.

SLIPCOVERS

Dining-Chair Cover

Update your old dining chairs with smart, new covers that fit over the padded seats. Use a red-and-white cotton toile de Jouy for a fresh, classic look that is easy to launder. For a neat fit, make a pattern before you begin. (See pages 198–199.)

YOU WILL NEED

- Main fabric—see right for estimating the yardage

- Hook-and-loop tape

- Matching sewing thread

- Small amount of cotton tape

ESTIMATING YARDAGE

- Make a pattern for the chair cover from muslin or calico following the instructions on pages 198–199.

- Using the pattern pieces, estimate the main fabric required, plus an extra amount for four ties, each 1½ x 14 inches.

1 From the main fabric, cut out one seat piece and one skirt piece, joining fabric widths together, if necessary, to achieve the required length. (See page 184.) With right sides together, pin and machine-stitch the corner darts in place at the front edges of the seat piece.

2 At the back, cut-away corners of the seat piece, work a row of machine stay stitching ⅝ inch from the raw edge, extending approximately 1¼ inches from each side of the corner. (See page 183.) Diagonally clip into the corner seam allowance, as shown.

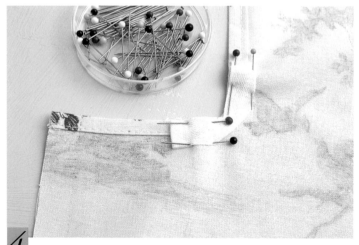

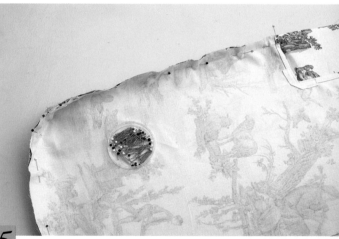

4 Pin a piece of cotton tape to the wrong side of the cut-away corner, enclosing the raw corner edges, by folding over the tape to make a right angle. Tuck under the raw ends, and machine-stitch along all edges of the tape.

5 With right sides together, matching the center fronts of both the seat and skirt piece, pin the top edge of the skirt around the front and side edges of the seat. The skirt should extend equally beyond the seat cut-away corners at both sides. Machine-stitch the skirt in place with a ⅝-inch seam allowance.

3 Press a double-fold ⁵⁄₁₆-inch hem to the wrong side along the straight back and cut-away edges of the seat piece. Pin and machine-stitch the hems in place.

TIP

This style dining-chair cover can be made with various skirt lengths; from short, as shown here, to floor length, which can be useful if chair legs need disguising. Just decide on your desired length and then cut the fabric accordingly.

6 Clip notches into the curved front corner seam allowances, snipping no closer than ⅛ inch from the stitching.

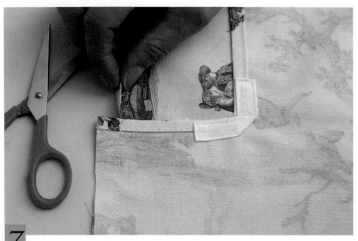

7 Clip into the skirt seam allowance at the beginning and end of the skirt seam where the back extensions start.

8 Press a double-fold ⁵⁄₁₆-inch hem onto the wrong side along the top edge of the skirt back extensions, down the short ends, and along the lower edge of the skirt. Pin and machine-stitch the hems in place.

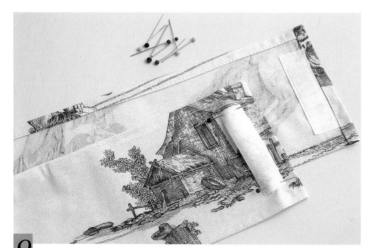

9 Cut a short length of hook-and-loop tape. Pin and machine-stitch the loop side of the tape onto the wrong side of one skirt back extension, placing it ¾ inch from the back edge. Pin and machine-stitch the hook side of the tape to the right side of the remaining skirt back extension in the same way to correspond.

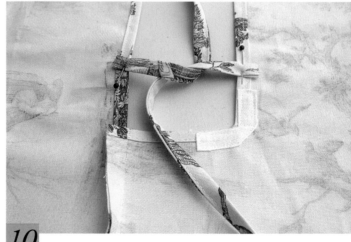

10 Following the instructions on page 188, make up four narrow ties. Place the cover over the chair seat and fasten the hook-and-loop tape. Flip the back of the seat piece over the top of the skirt extensions and mark the tie positions at either side of the back chair struts. Remove the cover and oversew the ties in place by hand. (See page 183.) Replace the cover on the chair, fastening the hook-and-loop tape again, and tie the ties in bows at the back corners.

A wooden country chair is given a striped seat cover that doesn't have to fit too neatly over a flat chair pad. There's no need to make a fitted pattern: you can work out the dimensions by measuring across the top and around the sides. Let the fabric hang down the back to cover the side flaps, and tie the cover to the chair legs with tapes.

Ruffle-Edged Chair Pad

Perfect for the country-style kitchen, this striped chair pad has been made with ruffled edges and ties to keep it in place. Choose a decorator fabric that is washable, hardwearing, and can withstand the constant wear-and-tear of everyday use.

YOU WILL NEED

- Main decorator fabric—see right for estimating the yardage

- Matching sewing thread

- Ready-made square or rectangular pillow form to fit your chair seat

- A zipper that is 3 inches shorter than the width of the pillow form

ESTIMATING YARDAGE

- Measure the length and width of the ready-made pillow form.

- For the top of the chair pad allow one piece of main fabric that is the size of the form, plus a ⅝-inch seam allowance around all sides.

- For the base of the chair pad, allow one piece of main fabric that is the size of the form and will be cut in half, plus a ⅝-inch seam allowance around all sides.

- For the ruffle, take the width of the pillow form, plus twice the length, and double the resulting measurement. Allow for the length of the ruffle strip, plus 1¼ inches for hem allowances, by 7½ inches deep. You will need to join fabric pieces to obtain the correct length for your ruffle, so allow an extra 1⅛ inches to the length of each fabric piece for seam allowances.

- Allow for four ties that are each 2⅜ x 10 inches.

1 From the fabric, cut out one top piece, two bottom pieces, and the ruffle pieces. With right sides facing, seam the ruffle strips together, with a ⅝-inch seam allowance. Press the seam allowances open.

2 With right sides together, fold the ruffle strip in half lengthwise. Pin and machine-stitch across both short ends, with a ⅝-inch seam allowance. Turn out the seamed ends to the right side, and carefully push out the corners with a pointed object, such as the points of a pair of scissors, to form neat points. Press the seamed edges flat, and then with long raw edges even, press the ruffle in half all along its length.

4 Place the ruffle on to the right side of the top piece, and with raw edges even, pin it in place along the front and side edges, starting and finishing ⅝ inch from the back edge. Baste the ruffle in place.

5 Machine-stitch the gathered ruffle around the front and side edges, with a ⅝-inch seam allowance. Remove the basting stitches.

3 Baste the raw edges of the ruffle together. Work two parallel rows of very large basting stitches along the raw edges of the ruffle, spacing them roughly a ¼ inch apart. Carefully pull the stitching end threads to gather the fabric evenly along the ruffle until it fits around the front and sides of the top piece.

6 With right sides together, pin and baste the two bottom pieces together along one long side. Machine-stitch the seam together for 1½ inches at either end, leaving the basting stitches in the center intact. Press open the seam, and insert the zipper, as shown on page 202. Remove the basting stitches. Place the bottom piece over the top piece, with right sides facing. Pin and machine-stitch the pieces together, with a ⅝-inch seam allowance, sandwiching the ruffle between them, and starting and finishing ⅝ inch from the back edge.

7 Press both the top and bottom seam allowances ⅝ inch onto the wrong side, along the back raw edges. Clip the seam allowances at the front corners and then turn the cover to the right side.

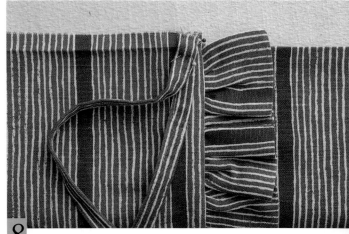

8 Make up the four ties. (See page 188.) Open the pressed back edge on the bottom, and with raw edges even, place two ties, one on top of the other, at each side edge of the back. Pin and baste the ties in place. Machine-stitch the ties in place along the press line, stitching over the same place several times to reinforce.

9 Remove the basting stitches, and fold the pressed seam allowances back to the wrong side, so that the ties face up. Open the zipper.

10 Pin and baste together the pressed-back edges, sandwiching the ties between them. Then machine-stitch the edges together, working close to the pressed edge. Insert the pillow form through the zipper opening, and fasten the zipper to close.

TIPS

• If you're pressed for time, here's an easier version of this chair pad. Cut the top and base pieces the same size and omit the zipper. The back edges are then left open and only slipstitched together once the pillow form has been inserted. It is fairly easy to remove the slipstitching and the pad whenever the covers need to be laundered.

• These slipcovers provide an easy way to update kitchen chairs and tie them in with a new color scheme. You could make several sets in fabrics to match the tablecloth, napkins, or the window shade or curtains.

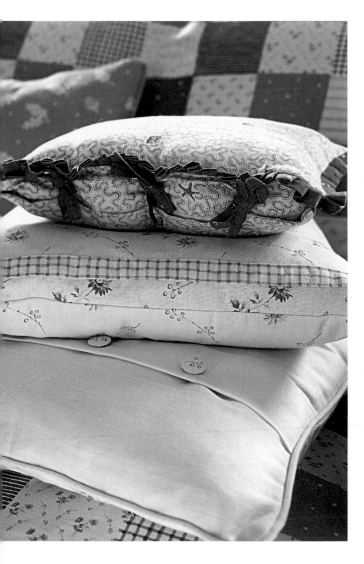

VARIATIONS

Using the technique explained in these steps, make a frill and use it for trimming pillows too. Gather a contrast-colored ruffle and fit it to the edge of a pretty pillow, or give a more formal look by pleating the strip to fit. Either way, you can give your home a personalized look that will fit in beautifully with any type of scheme.

Slipper-Chair Cover

It's amazing how you can change the look of an old, junk-store chair with a crisp linen cover. This chair was frayed and worn out, but the new cover revealed its lovely proportions. Now, it's a useful and decorative piece of furniture for a bedroom.

YOU WILL NEED

- Main decorator fabric—see below for yardage
- Drapery lining—see right for yardage
- Matching sewing thread
- Medium-sized cable cord—see right for yardage
- Hook-and-loop tape—see right for yardage

ESTIMATING YARDAGE

- For the seat section: measure the depth over the top of the seat from front to back, and add 1¼ inches for seam allowances, plus 2½ inches for a tuck-in at the back. Measure across the width of the seat and add 1¼ inches for seams.

- For the inside back piece: measure the length of the inside back from the top back edge down the front of the back to the seat, and add 1¼ inches for seams, plus an extra 2½ inches for a tuck-in at the base. Measure the width of the inside back from one side back edge, across the front to the opposite side back edge. Take this measurement at both the top and base of the inside back, in case the back of the chair tapers, and add 1¼ inches for seam allowances.

- For the back piece: measure the depth of the pleated skirt and place a line of pins around the chair at this point. Measure the length of the back from the pin line up to the top back edge of the chair. Measure the width of the chair back at both the top and the bottom in case the back tapers and add a ⅝-inch seam allowance to all sides.

- For the box edging piece: measure around the sides of the seat from the back edge, across the front, to the opposite back edge; add 1¼ inches for seams. For the depth, measure from the pin-line up to the top of the seat at the front and back edges of the chair, as the piece may need to taper; add 1¼ inches for seams.

- For the pleated skirt: measure around the pin line, and add 10 inches for each pleat. Measure the depth for the skirt from the pin line down to the floor, plus ⅜ inch. Add a ⅝-inch seam allowance to all sides. Join fabric widths, if necessary, to obtain the correct length. (See page 184.)

- For the lining, you will need the same size as calculated for the pleated skirt, but take off ⅜ inch from the depth measurement.

- For the cable cord, you will need enough to go around all the edges of the back piece and both edges of the seat box edging, plus 8 inches.

- For covering the cable cord, first gauge the width of your fabric strip. To do this, measure around the cord and add 1¼ inches for seam allowances. (See page 186.) Allow enough bias-grain strips of fabric to fit the length of your cable cord.

- For the hook-and-loop tape, measure the length from 2 inches below the top of the chair to the bottom edge of the skirt.

1 From the main fabric, cut out a back, a seat, an inside back, a box edge piece, and a skirt. Cut one skirt piece from the lining fabric. With the wrong side facing up, place the inside back piece on the chair, and fold and pin the top two corners to fit over the top edge. Remove the fabric piece and machine-stitch the darts in place.

2 Fold the inside back piece in half along its lower edge and mark the center point with a pin. Fold the back edge of the seat piece in half and mark the center with a pin. Place the seat piece on top of the inside back, with pins matching, and mark the side edges of the seat with more pins. Remove the seat piece and set to one side. To form the tuck-in sections on the lower edge of the inside back, pin a curved shape no deeper than 2½ inches from the pin at the bottom left-hand corner, as shown.

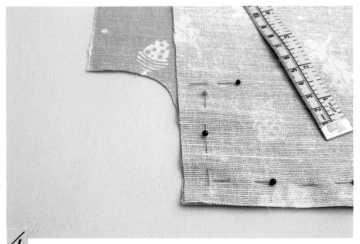

4 With right sides together, place the seat piece back on top of the inside back, matching the center pins and the side edges to the curved tuck-in sections. Pin the pieces together along the back edge and up both sides of the tuck-in sections for a depth of 2½ inches. Machine-stitch the pieces together with a ⅝-inch seam allowance.

5 With right sides facing, seam the cable cord strips together to obtain the correct length required for covering the cord, and make up the cording as shown on page 186. With right sides facing up, pin and baste the cording to the top edge of the seat's box-edging piece, keeping raw edges even. Using a zipper foot on your machine, stitch the cording in place, working as close to the cord as possible. Mark the positions of the seat front corners on both the top and bottom edges of the box-edging piece, with hand-sewn tailor's tacks. (See page 181.)

3 Trim away the fabric following the pin line, and repeat at the bottom right-hand corner of the inside back.

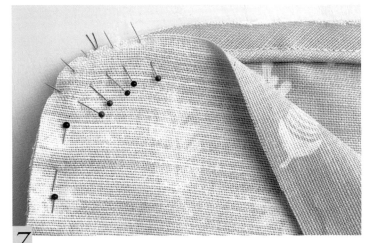

6 Using scissors, gently curve the two front pointed corners of the seat piece, as shown.

7 With right sides together, pin the corded edge of the box-edging piece to the seat and the remaining curved edges of the inside back tuck-in sections. Baste the pieces together. Working with the box-edging piece on top and using a zipper foot on your machine, stitch the pieces together by re-stitching over the cording stitch line, making sure to get as close to the cord as possible.

TIP

When making tailored slipcovers, it is always best to first cut out a pattern from plain cotton and sew it together, omitting the cording. This way you can check the fit and make sure you are happy with it before you begin for real. Doing this will avoid making any expensive mistakes caused by cutting your chosen fabric incorrectly.

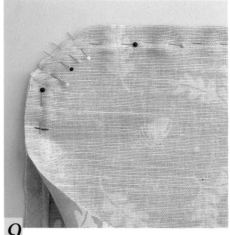

8 Round off the top pointed corners of the back piece. With right sides up, pin, baste, and machine-stitch the cording to the top and side edges of the back, as shown in step 5. With right sides facing, pin the corded back to the edges of the inside back, leaving the left-hand side edges open, 2 inches below the top edge of the chair to the bottom.

9 Stitch the pieces together as shown for the cording in step 7. At the right-hand side edge of the back piece, continue stitching down to the lower edge joining it to the short back edge of the box-edging piece.

10 To make the pleated skirt, join the fabric pieces to obtain the correct skirt width. Line the skirt as shown in steps 2, 3, 4, and 5 of "Pleated Dust Ruffle", on pages 132–133. At each short end of the skirt, fold half an inverted pleat 2½ inches deep, and pin in place. The edges of this pleat will butt together when the left-hand back opening edges are closed.

11 Fold over and pin three 5-inch-wide inverted pleats in the skirt, to correspond with each of the two front corners of the seat and the remaining back corner. (See page 190.) Pin the skirt around the bottom edge of the chair cover, and adjust the pleats, if necessary, to fit. Baste the pleats in place.

12 Stitch a length of cording to the top edge of the skirt, as shown in step 5. To finish the ends, trim the cording about ⅝ inch beyond the ends of the skirt. Rip out about 2 inches of the cording stitches; trim away the uncovered cable cord level with the ends of the skirt and fold the covering strip back to neaten. Pin in place.

13 With right sides facing, pin and machine-stitch the top edge of the skirt to the lower edge of the back and seat box-edging piece, as shown for the cording in step 7, placing the short ends of the skirt ⅝ inch from the left-hand side back opening edges, and matching the front and back seams to the pleat centers.

14 Pin the hook section of the hook-and-loop tape to the wrong side of the opening on the back piece, butting the edge of the tape up to the cording. Machine-stitch the tape in place from the top of the opening to the skirt. Take the work out of the machine and rejoin the seam below the cording for the skirt. Continue to stitch to the bottom of the skirt. Repeat on the other edge of the opening, stitching the loop side of the tape to the right side of the inside back and seat box-edging piece. Turn the cover to the right side, place over the chair, tucking the fabric in the back of the seat. Close the tape openings.

VARIATIONS

Above left: A fitted cover looks just as good without the pleated skirt. Everything else is made in the same way, but the look is more tailored, and has an elegance that is suited to a formal scheme.

Above: Another variation is to omit the box-edging piece and stitch the pleated skirt directly onto the seat, inside back, and back pieces.

Tied Dining-Chair Cover

Transform your dining chairs for the summer months with fresh, brightly colored covers that slip easily over the top of formal winter upholstery. Made from rectangles of fabric, the cover is fastened at the back with a large bow, to create a soft yet elegant look.

YOU WILL NEED

- Main decorator fabric—see right for estimating the yardage

- Matching sewing thread

ESTIMATING YARDAGE

- For the front of the chair cover, measure the chair from the top down the back, along the seat, and down to the floor. Add 1⅜ inches to the measurement for a seam and hem allowance. Measure the width of the chair and add 1¼ inches for seam allowances. Allow for one piece of fabric the length calculated, by the width.

- For the back of the cover, measure the chair from the top down to the floor and add 1⅜ inches to the measurement for a seam and hem allowance. Measure the width of the chair back and add 32 inches to the measurement for an inverted pleat plus 1¼ inches for seam allowances. (See page 190.) Allow for one piece of fabric the length by the width.

- For the chair sides, measure the height from the seat to the floor and add 1⅜ inches to the measurement for a seam and hem allowance. Measure the width of the chair sides, from leg to leg, and add 1¼ inches for seam allowances. Allow for two pieces of fabric the height by the width.

- For the bow, you will need to allow two straight-grain pieces of fabric, 5 x 27½ inches.

1 From the fabric, cut out one back, one front, and two side pieces, plus two bow strips. With right sides together, place one side piece onto the front piece, aligning the bottom and right side edges. Pin the pieces together with a ⅝-inch seam allowance, stopping ⅝ inch before the top edge of the side piece.

2 Machine-stitch the pieces together, and clip into the seam allowance of the long front piece, at the point where the stitching ends, as shown.

5 Mark the center point along the top and bottom edges of the back piece with pins and press in a 16-inch wide inverted pleat down the center back. (See page 190.) Pin and baste the pleat in place, through all layers of fabric, at the top edge.

6 With right sides facing, place the joined front and side pieces on top of the back piece. Pin the pieces together along the side edges, folding the extra seat fabric out of the way, as shown.

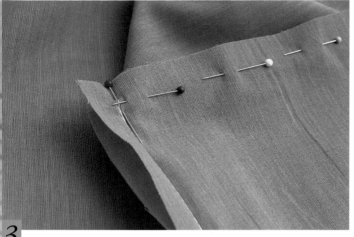

3 Fold the front piece at the clipped seam turning and pin it along the top edge of the side piece, finishing ⅝ inch before the end of the side piece. Machine-stitch the pieces together. Repeat steps 1, 2, and 3 with the remaining side piece and the left edge of the front piece.

4 Clip into the seam allowances on both edges of the long front piece at the point where the stitching ends on the top edge of the side pieces, as shown.

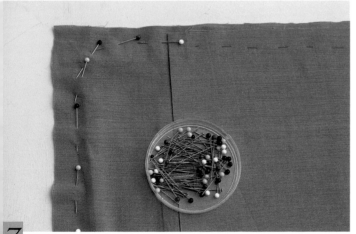

7 Pin the remaining top edges of the cover together, curving the corners slightly to fit your chair back. Machine-stitch the pieces together around the top and side edges with a ⅝-inch seam allowance.

8 Clip into the seam turnings, no closer than ⅛ inch to the stitching line, around the corners to create smooth curves when the cover is turned to the right side.

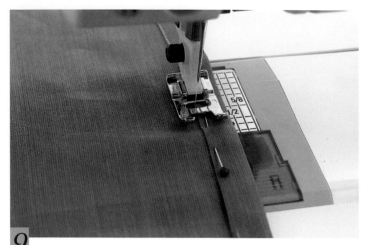

9 Press a double-fold ⅜-inch hem to the wrong side along the bottom edges of the cover. Pin and machine-stitch the hem in place.

10 Turn the cover to the right side and carefully press all the seamed edges flat. Make up the two bow pieces as shown for narrow ties on page 188.

11 Press a 1-inch hem onto the wrong side at the raw end of each bow. On the right side of the cover, measure halfway down the back pleat and mark the pressed edges with pins. Open the pleat at one pin position and place the pressed end of a bow to it, overlapping the pleat edge by about 1¼ inches, as shown. Pin and machine-stitch the bow in place through all layers of fabric, working a cross-shape across the center to reinforce the stitching. Repeat with the remaining bow piece and side of the pleat, making sure the bows are level. Place the cover over the chair and tie the bows.

VARIATION

A weathered metal garden chair is given a quick makeover with a simple cover made in a fresh floral cotton fabric. Instead of a pleat at the back, leave the back edges open and join the sides with pairs of narrow ties.

TIP

Make a cover with a contrast-colored bow and backing. Cut the back in two pieces, half the width of the chair back, plus 9¼ inches for the pleat and seams. Cut a 17¼-inch-wide contrast pleat backing. Make the cover as above, but seam the back pieces together to form one panel, with the contrast strip running down the center, before starting step 5.

Tailored Armchair Cover

Make a cover for a favorite but worn armchair and give it a new lease on life. This cover uses a piece of antique linen with the original cross-stitch monograms placed on the arm fronts, but any hardwearing linen or linen union would be suitable. If your chair has a seat cushion, see "Shaped Box-Edged Cushions" on pages 100–103 for instructions.

YOU WILL NEED

- Main decorator fabric—see right for estimating yardage

- Matching sewing thread

- Medium-sized cable cord—see right for estimating yardage

- Hook-and-loop tape—see right for estimating yardage

ESTIMATING YARDAGE

- For the main fabric, follow the step-by-step instructions for "Making a pattern for an armchair" on pages 192–197.

- For the cable cord, you will need enough to go around the front edges of the arms, plus 2 inches extra.

- For covering the cable cord, first gauge the width of your fabric strip. To do this, measure around the cord and add an extra 1 ½ inches for seam allowances. (See page 186.) Allow enough bias-grain strips of fabric in this width to fit the length of your cable cord.

- You will need a piece of hook-and-loop tape to fit the height of the chair back.

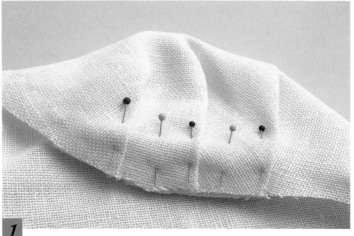

1 Cut out one outer back piece, one inner back piece, one seat piece, two inside arm pieces, two outside arm pieces, two front arm pieces, and one front box-edging piece. Measure and mark a tuck-in allowance of 4 inches with a line of contrast basting stitches along the back and side edges of the seat piece, the lower edge of the inner back piece, and along the lower edge of the inside arm pieces. Place the inner back piece in position on the chair and fold and pin small pleats at the top corner edges, shaping the fabric to fit over the curved top edges of the chair.

2 Remove the inner back piece from the chair. Baste the pleats in place around the curved shapes at each top corner of the inner back piece, removing the pins as you work.

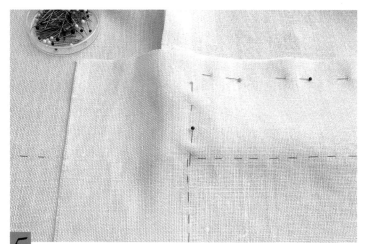

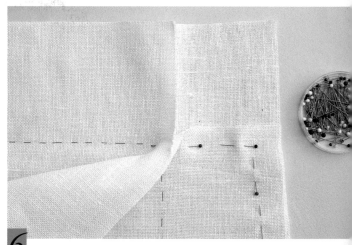

5 Align the lower edge of the inner back to the back edge of the seat piece, with right sides together, leaving 3⅛ inches of the seat piece extending at each side. Pin the pieces together with a ¾-inch seam allowance. Working with the seat piece on top, pin the edges of the inner back tuck-in allowance to the seat piece, starting at the corners of the contrast basted lines and ending at the previous pinned edge. Repeat for the opposite side. Machine-stitch the tuck-in seams along the pinned lines.

6 Pin and machine-stitch the lower edges of the inside arm pieces to the side edges of the seat piece and across the tuck-in allowances, as shown in step 5 for the inner back.

3 With right sides together, pin the top edge of the outer back piece to the top curved edge of the inner back piece, starting and finishing at the last pleat on each side. Machine-stitch the pieces together with a ¾-inch seam allowance.

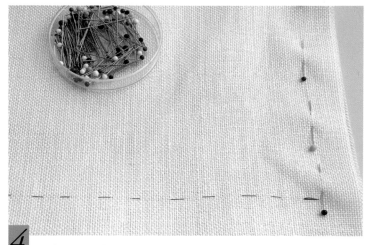

4 With right sides together, pin the back edge of one inside arm piece to one side edge of the inner back piece, matching the basted tuck-in lines. Machine-stitch the pieces with a ¾-inch seam allowance, starting at the basted lines and finishing ¾-inch from the top edge of the inside arm piece. Repeat with the other side and the remaining inside arm piece.

7 At each back corner, carefully trim away the excess square of fabric from the tuck-in allowance, as shown.

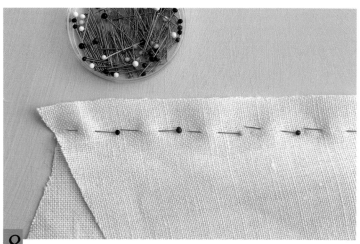

8 Pin the top edge of one the inside arm piece to the top edge of one outside arm piece. Machine-stitch the pieces together with a ¾-inch seam allowance. Repeat for the other side with the remaining outside arm piece.

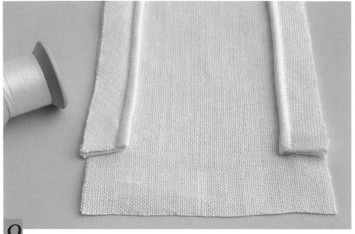

9 With right sides facing, seam together the cable cord strips to obtain the correct length required for covering the cord. (See page 187.) Make up the cording as shown on page 186. With right sides up, pin and baste the cording to one front arm piece, keeping the raw edges even. To finish the ends, trim the cording level with the bottom edge of the front arm piece. Rip out about 2½ inches of the cording stitching; trim away 1½ inches of the uncovered cable cord and fold the covering strip back over to neaten, as shown. Pin in place.

10 Using a zipper foot on your machine, stitch the cording in place, working as close to the cord as possible. Repeat for the other front arm piece. Clip notches around the curved seam allowances of the arm pieces and cording.

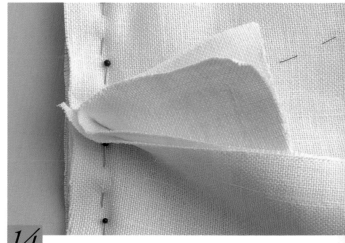

13 With right sides together, and starting and finishing at the lower edge, pin and baste the joined outside arms, inside arms, and front box-edging pieces to the corded front arms, easing the fullness around the top as you go.

14 Using a zipper foot on your machine, stitch the pieces together by stitching over the cording stitch line, making sure you get as close to the cord as possible. When stitching up to the projecting tuck-in, reverse-stitch to secure and remove the work from the machine. Replace the work the other side of the tuck-in and continue stitching as before.

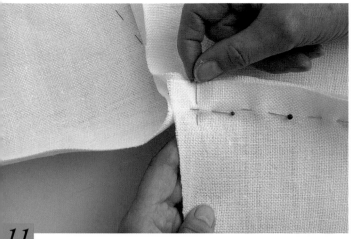

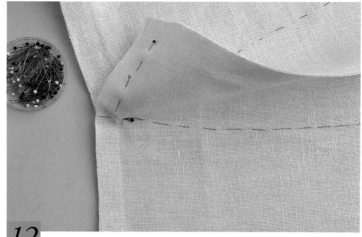

11 Align the top edge of the front box-edging piece to the front edge of the seat piece, with right sides together and 3⅛ inches of the seat piece extending at each side. Pin the pieces together with a ¾-inch seam allowance. Machine-stitch the pieces starting and finishing ¾ inch in from the side edges of the box-edging piece.

12 Stitch the front edge of one inside arm to the front edge of the seat piece across the tuck-in section, with a ¾-inch seam allowance. Repeat with the other inside arm front edge.

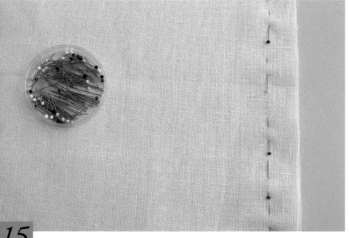

15 With right sides facing, pin the outer back piece to the right-hand back edge of the joined outside and inside arm pieces. Start at the inner back shaping pleats and end at the lower hem edge. Machine-stitch the pieces with a ¾-inch seam allowance. On the left-hand side of the outer back, pin and machine-stitch the pieces from the lower edge of the inner back, shaping pleats for about 2 inches, leaving the seam open below.

16 Neaten all seams, except the lower edge, with a machine zigzag stitch, or use a serger. Press a ¾-inch double-fold hem to the wrong side along the lower edge. Pin and machine-stitch in place. Separate the hook-and-loop tape and pin the hook section to the wrong side of the opening on the outer back piece; machine-stitch in place from the hem to the top of the opening. Repeat with the loop side along the other edge of the opening, stitching it to the right side of the fabric. Turn the cover to the right side and press. Pull the cover over the chair, and close the opening. Replace the cushion.

VARIATIONS

These photos show how you can make a sofa cover in the same way as the armchair cover on the previous pages. Simply extend the pattern across the center. The fabric will need to be joined, so either make a seam down the center or add a central panel and seam part-panels on either side. Adding cording to all the seams will strengthen them.

If you want to fit a skirt with inverted pleats at the corners, measure and allow for a pleated skirt as on pages 34–39 and follow steps 10, 11, 12, and 13.

If your sofa seat cushions are shaped around the arms, follow the instructions for the shaped box-edged cushion featured on pages 100–103.

Arm Cover

Protect the arms of a favorite upholstered chair with fabric covers. If possible, make the covers from the same fabric as the upholstery. Otherwise, choose a complementary solid color or something to match your throw pillows. If the covers become soiled, they slip off easily for cleaning. Just be sure to pre-shrink the fabric beforehand.

YOU WILL NEED

- Main decorator fabric—see right for estimating the yardage

- Medium-sized cable cord—see right for estimating the yardage

- Matching sewing thread

- Paper for making a pattern

ESTIMATING YARDAGE

- Make a paper pattern for the arm front. To do this, decide on how far down you want the cover to sit. Mark the positions with pins on the inside and outside of the arm and at the front edge (make sure the pins are at a level height). Place the paper over the arm front, and trace around the edge starting and finishing at the pins. Remove the tracing, neaten the curves, and join the two ends of the line together, to form a horizontal base. Add a 5⁄8-inch seam allowance around all sides, and cut out the pattern piece. You will need one pair of front arms for each chair.

- For the arm cover top, measure around the traced line on the front cover, excluding the lower edge, to find the length. For the width, decided how far along the arm you want the cover to sit. Draw a rectangular pattern piece to these measurements, adding a 5⁄8-inch seam allowance around all edges. You will need two top pieces for each chair.

- For the cable cord, you will need enough to go around the edges of each front cover, excluding the lower edges.

- For covering the cable cord, first gauge the width of your fabric strip. To do this, measure around the cord and allow an extra 1 1⁄4 inches for seam allowances. Allow enough bias-grain strips of fabric of this width, to fit the length of your cable cord. (See page 186.)

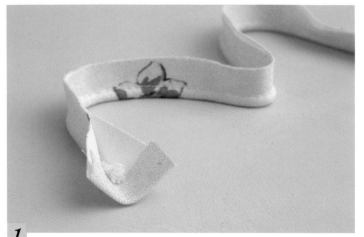

1 Cut out the front, top, and cable-cord covering pieces from the main fabric. Make up the cording as shown on pages 186–187. Neaten one end of the cording by undoing 2 inches of stitching. Trim the fabric end and press over a ⅜-inch hem onto the wrong side. Cut the cable cord to within ⅜ inch of the pressed edge. Wrap the strip back around the cord, and pin and machine-stitch it in place.

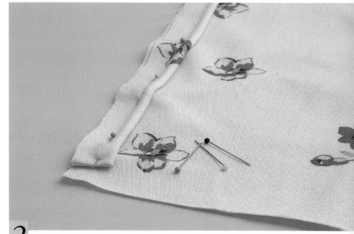

2 Position the cording on the right side of one front piece, ⅝ inch up from the lower edge, with raw edges even. Pin the cording in place around the curved edge, easing the cording around the top curves and ending ⅝ inch from the lower edge on the other side. Neaten the end of the cording as shown in step 1. Baste the cording in place.

5 Neaten all the raw edges with a machine zigzag stitch, or use a serger if you own one. Turn the cover to the right side and press the seamed edges. Press a ⅝-inch hem to the wrong side along the remaining straight edges.

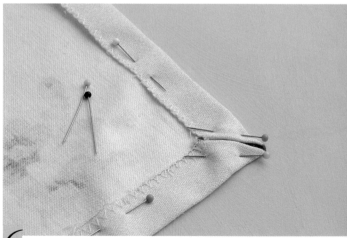

6 Miter the corners of the hems. (See page 191.) Pin and machine-stitch the hems in place, working ⅜ inch from the pressed edge. Repeat steps 2, 3, 4, 5, and 6 with the remaining arm cover pieces.

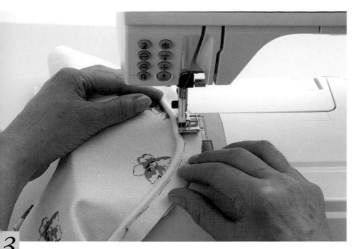

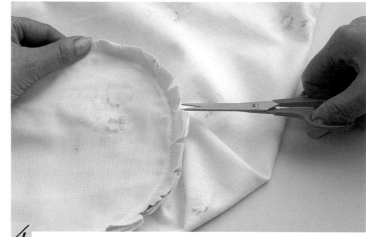

3 Using the zipper foot on your machine, stitch the cording to the front piece, re-stitching over the cording stitch line. Make sure to get as close to the cord as possible. Remove the basting stitches.

4 With right sides together and with raw edges even, pin the rectangular top piece to the corded edge of the front piece. Baste the pieces together. Working with the front piece on top, machine-stitch the pieces together as shown in step 3. Remove the basting stitches, and clip the curved seam allowance.

VARIATION

The arms of this upholstered sofa are narrower and less rounded than the main project, but making your own paper pattern means that you can adapt the method to any shape. It's a good idea to use arm covers because they will prolong the life of the fabric underneath.

TIP

Make more than one set of arm covers and have a new pair ready when you pop the originals in the laundry. This will also prevent the fabric colors fading too quickly.

New-Look Antimacassar

A quick and easy way to create a different look in the sitting room is to throw an interesting panel over the back of the sofa. Find a fabric that has plenty of surface texture, like this ready-quilted material, and neaten the edges with iron-on hemming web for a brilliant no-sew idea. The antimacassar was originally used in the early years of the twentieth century to protect chair backs from gentlemen's "Macassar" hair oil, but this contemporary version brings the idea up to date.

VARIATION

For an instant way to protect the seat or back of a chair, why not simply use a softly-colored woollen blanket neatly folded over the seat? Find one that works with the colors of the pillows, and it becomes a part of the scheme.

Bound-Edged Throw

One of the easiest ways to change a room is to drape a richly colored throw over a sofa. This throw is made from a luxurious, double-sided fabric that looks good from both sides. It has been edged with a golden-colored linen binding for a sumptuous appearance.

- 1¾ yards of main fabric

- Contrast fabric for the bound edge—see right for estimating the yardage

- Matching sewing thread

- Dressmakers' chalk

- Measuring tape and ruler

- A triangle, or similar right-angled item

- Square off the cut ends of the main fabric piece, using the triangle, ruler, and dressmakers' chalk. Cut the fabric along the chalk lines, and neatly trim away the selvages down each edge. Measure the width and length of the resulting fabric piece.

- For the binding strips, allow two strips of contrast fabric 6 inches wide, by the length of the main fabric piece, and two strips 6 inches wide, by the width of the main fabric piece, plus 1¼ inches for the hem allowances. Note: To save fabric, you can cut each side binding in two pieces and seam them together to form the full lengths.

1 Using the dressmakers' chalk and a ruler, lightly draw a border 1¾ inches from the outer edge, all around the main fabric piece, on the right side.

2 From the contrast fabric, cut out the binding strip pieces. Seam the side pieces together, if you have cut them in two. Press a ⅝-inch hem onto the wrong side along one long edge of a side-binding strip.

3 With right sides facing, place the long raw edge of a side binding along the chalked line on the main fabric piece, lining up the short raw ends with the top and bottom edges. Pin the binding strip in place.

4 Machine-stitch the binding in place, stitching ⅝ inch from the raw edge of the strip.

5 Fold the binding strip back over toward the side, and then press the turnings toward the binding strip.

6 Fold the pressed edge of the binding strip over the edge and onto the wrong side of the main fabric. Position the pressed edge just over the machine-stitched line and pin and baste it in place.

TIP

For a quick and easy way to finish off the edges of a throw, simply press over and machine-stitch a neat hem all around the outside edges of the main fabric. Alternatively, use a ready-made binding, ribbon, or braid in a complementary or contrasting color to decorate the edges.

VARIATION

Choose a beautiful woven fabric with a strong pattern. Edge it with a solid color for a sofa throw that will really make a statement. Adding a large tassel to each corner will give it even more impact, especially if you make a pillow cover to match.

7 On the right side of the main fabric piece, machine-stitch the binding in place through all layers of fabric, stitching close to the binding edge along the basted line. Make sure to tuck in the hem. Remove the basting stitches and press the bound edge. Repeat the stitching with the opposite side edge and binding strip.

8 Press over a ⅝-inch hem onto the wrong side along one long edge, and across the short ends of the top and bottom binding strips.

9 Stitch the top binding strip to the top edge of the main fabric piece and the bottom binding strip to the bottom edge, as shown in steps 3 to 7. Overlap the ends of the side bindings and line up the short pressed ends with the finished edges of the throw. Close the open ends of the top and bottom bindings with a hand slipstitch. (See page 183.)

Sofa Update

Disguise an out-dated sofa with a quilted cotton throw-over cover, to hide worn areas or marks, or to conceal old-fashioned upholstery. It is a simple yet very effective tonic for a tired sitting room. For a cover that is slightly more fitted, hand-stitch cotton tapes in a coordinating color along the folds at each side, and tie them together to hold the cover in place. Tuck any excess fabric neatly down the sides of the seating box pillows, and you will have an instant sofa makeover.

VARIATION

Use leather thongs rather than cotton tapes for a more contemporary look. These work well with textured fabrics, such as heavyweight linen.

Garden-Chair Pad and Glider-Cover

Metal folding chairs can be uncomfortable to sit on for any length of time, so make some welcoming striped tie-on chair pads for the seats and slip-on glider-covers for the backs. Use a heavyweight cotton, canvas, or outdoor fabric for garden chairs.

YOU WILL NEED

- Main decorator fabric—see right for estimating yardage

- Matching sewing thread

- ⅜-inch thick, high-density, flame-retardant foam or thin batting—see right for estimating the yardage

ESTIMATING YARDAGE

- For the chair pad, measure the depth of the seat from back to front, and add 2 inches for the front fold-back, plus 1½ inches for the hems. Measure the width of the seat from side to side, and add 3 inches for the side overlaps, plus 1½ inches for seam allowances. Allow for one piece of main fabric.

- For the ties, you will need four 3 x 23½-inch bias or straight-grain strips of main fabric.

- For the glider-cover, measure the depth of the chair back, double it, and add 1½ inches for hem allowances. Measure the width of the chair back and add 1½ inches for seam allowances. Allow for one piece of main fabric.

- You will need the same amount of foam, or batting, as calculated for the chair pad and glider-cover main fabric pieces.

1 Cut out one chair pad piece, one glider-cover piece, and four ties from the main fabric. From the foam, or batting, cut out one chair pad piece and one glider-cover piece. Place the glider-cover fabric piece on a flat surface with the wrong side facing up, and lay the foam or batting on top, with the raw edges even.

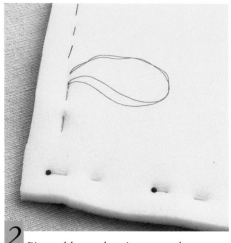

2 Pin and baste the pieces together around all the edges with a 1-inch seam allowance.

3 Trim away the foam or batting to within ¼ inch of the basting stitches along the top and bottom edges, as shown.

5 With right sides together, fold the glider-cover in half with the hemmed edges level. Pin, baste, and machine-stitch the side seams together with a ⅝-inch seam allowance. If you find it difficult to machine-stitch foam, join the side edges together using hand-sewn backstitch.

6 Using a sharp pair of scissors, carefully trim the foam or batting away from the seam allowances, as before.

7 Turn the glider-cover right side out, and lightly press. Slip the cover over the back of the chair.

TIP

If your garden chairs are old and likely to snag the foam or batting, line the backs with a plain cotton fabric. Simply cut the lining fabric to the same size as the foam or batting, and sandwich the foam or batting in-between the two layers.

VARIATION

Mix and match projects, like the frilled dining-chair seat and the back of the garden chair, to make a much dressier cover for a simple chair. Take it outside on a sunny day, but it's pretty enough for a dining room too.

4 Turn up a double-fold ⅜-inch hem along the top and lower edges, enclosing the raw edge of the foam or batting. Pin, baste, and machine-stitch the hems in place, close to the inner pressed edges. Remove the basting stitches.

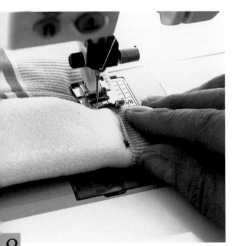

8 To make the chair pad, follow steps 1, 2, 3, and 4 to neaten all four sides of the pad. Then fold the front edge 2 inches onto the right side, and pin in place. Machine stitch the fold-back in place with a ⅝-inch seam allowance.

9 Turn the fold-back right side out and press. If you have used foam to line your pad, take care not to melt it with the hot iron.

10 Make up four ties, as on page 188. Pin the ties along the hemmed back edge, placing the first one in line with one side edge, and the second 1½ inches from the edge. Repeat at the opposite side. Machine-stitch the ties in place. Place the chair pad on the seat, slipping the fold-back over the front edge. Tie to secure.

Box-Edged Stool Cover

Look out for an old stool at a thrift store or garage sale. Cover it with a smart new striped cover that ties together at the corners. It will make a handy seat for the bathroom, as well as a useful surface on which to keep toiletries within comfortable reach of your luxurious bubble bath!

YOU WILL NEED

- Main decorator fabric—see right for estimating the yardage

- Matching sewing thread

- A piece of high-density, flame-retardant foam, approximately 4-inches thick—see right for estimating the yardage

- Utility or craft knife

- Instant contact adhesive

ESTIMATING YARDAGE

- For the foam, measure the length and the width of the stool top.

- For the top fabric piece, measure the length, and width of the stool top, and add 1⅛ inches to each measurement for seam allowances.

- For the boxing strips, allow two strips that measure the length of the stool, and two strips the width of the stool, plus 1⅛ inches for seam allowances, by the depth of the foam 4 inches, plus 1⅛ inches for seam allowances.

- For the skirt pieces, measure from the top of the stool to the floor, and add 2½ inches for a seam and hem allowance. Allow for two skirt pieces the width of the stool, and two pieces the length of the stool, plus 3¾ inches for hem allowances, by the depth calculated.

- For the ties, allow eight 1½ x 12-inch straight-grain fabric strips.

PREPARATION

Cut out one top piece, four boxing strips, four skirts, and eight tie strips from the main fabric. Using a sharp utility or craft knife, cut the foam to size, and glue it to the top of the stool using the adhesive.

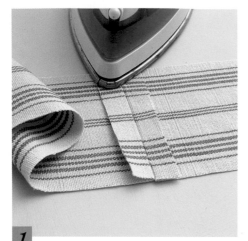

1 With right sides facing, pin the short edges of the boxing strips together to form a single ring. Machine-stitch the seams, with a ⅝-inch seam allowance, starting and finishing ⅝-inch from each edge. Press the seams open.

2 With right sides facing, and raw edges aligned, pin the joined boxing strips to the top piece, matching the seams to the corners. At each corner, the seam allowances on the boxing strips should be open, to help you turn the corner.

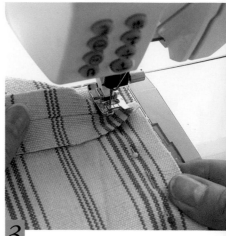

3 Taking a ⅝-inch seam allowance, machine-stitch the boxing strips to the top piece, removing the pins as you stitch. Trim away the seam allowance at the corners to reduce bulk and form neat corners.

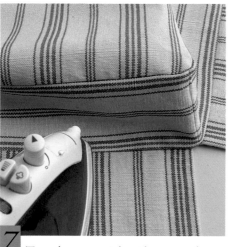

7 Turn the cover right side out, and press the seamed edges flat. Make up eight ties, as shown on page 188.

8 Pin the ties to the wrong side of the skirt, positioning one halfway down the sides of each skirt. Make sure each pair of ties are level, then machine-stitch or hand catch-stitch them in place. (See page 182.) Fit the cover over the stool and fashion the ties into bows.

TIP

An electric carving knife is handy for cutting through thick, high-density foam. Make sure you don't damage the surface beneath the foam when cutting it to size.

VARIATION

Instead of leaving the sides unstitched and closing them with ties, you could add a neat pleat at each corner. (See page 190.) This is useful if you wish to hide a less-than-lovely stool.

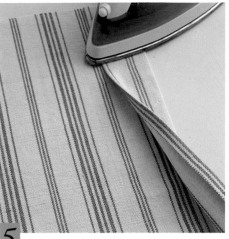

4 Press a ⅜-inch hem to the wrong side along the lower edge on each skirt piece, then press over another 1½-inch hem. Pin and machine-stitch in place.

5 Press a hem along both side edges of each skirt piece, as shown in step 4, pin, and machine-stitch in place.

6 With right sides together, place the top raw edge of each skirt piece to the corresponding raw edges of the boxing strips. Pin and machine-stitch in place with a ⅝-inch seam allowance.

Lace-Up Seat Cover

You won't need to sew a stitch if you want to make a new cover for a chair frame like this! A metal grommet kit makes short work of finishing off a length of narrow canvas, to replace the worn-out old cover. Measure carefully around your chair frame (using the photograph as a guide), and cut the canvas to fit, adding 2 inches at each end for hems. Press over a 1-inch double-fold hem at each end and insert the grommets, spaced evenly along the hems. Wrap the fabric around the chair frame and lace the ends together with cord. Tie the cord ends firmly together to secure.

VARIATIONS

Wooden deckchair frames can be re-covered in a similar way to make elegant and practical outdoor seating. Use good quality canvas or strong linen panels and lace them together around the frame, or simply double-stitch wide hems for the wooden battens to slot through.

CUSHIONS AND PILLOWS

The Easiest Pillow

When you want to update the look of a room in just an evening, there is no better way than to make a decorative pillow cover in your favorite fabric. This is an easy project—you don't even need a zipper. If you have never made a pillow cover before, this is the place to start!

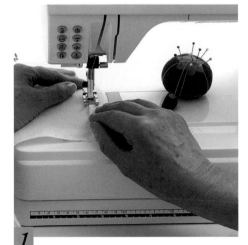

1 Cut one front piece of fabric that is 21¼ inches square, and two 21¼ x 15-inch back pieces. Press a 1-inch hem onto the wrong side and down one long edge of each back piece, then press over another 1 inch to the wrong side. Pin and machine-stitch the hems in place, stitching close to the first pressed edges.

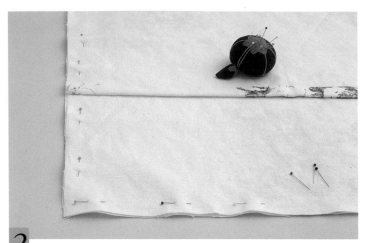

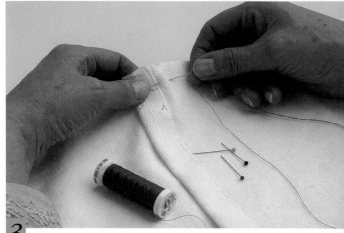

2 Lay the front piece right side up on a flat surface, then place the back covers on top, right sides down, with raw edges even and the hemmed edges overlapping at the center. Pin the pieces together around all four sides.

3 Baste the three pieces of fabric together around all the outer edges.

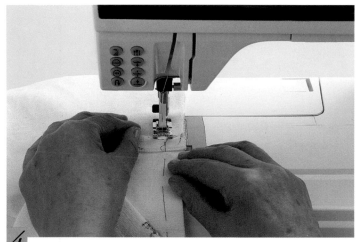

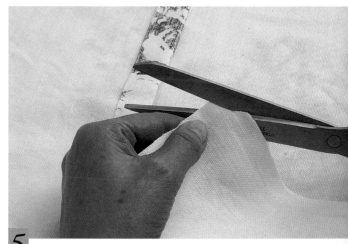

4 Machine-stitch around all four sides taking a ⅝-inch seam allowance. Remove the basting stitches.

5 Trim the seam allowances to ⅜ inch, and clip across the corners to make a better point. Turn the pillow cover right side out. Push out the corners and press the seamed edges flat. Insert the pillow form through the back opening, and smooth the back overlaps flat.

TIPS

• Strengthen the corners and the opening edges of the cover, by stitching over the first row of machine stitching all around the cover before turning it through to the right side.

• To help you form better corners, gently push the points of a pair of scissors into the corners when you have turned the cover through to the right side.

Left: Turn the pillow over and add buttons and buttonholes to the wrapped edge to accent it. Mixing a variety of stripe widths, all in the same two colors, is an interesting way of using pattern in a room.

Below left: Recycle a striped woollen blanket and turn it into a warm and cozy pillow for winter evenings. Make the most of the faded stripes by using them vertically and horizontally, and use the buttonhole-stitched edge as a hem.

81

Monogrammed Pillow

You can often find beautiful linen sheets at antique fairs. Make the most of an exquisite, hand-embroidered monogram when you give it pride of place on an heirloom pillow cover.

YOU WILL NEED

- Vintage monogrammed linen sheet

- Matching sewing thread

- Paper for making the pattern pieces

- 17¾-inch ready-made square pillow form

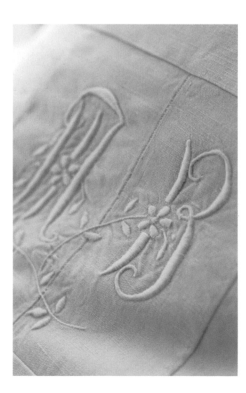

MAKING PAPER PATTERNS

- For the front, cut a paper pattern 17¾-inch square. Divide the square equally into three with two horizontal pencil lines, and cut out. Retain one of the resulting rectangles for the top and bottom panels. Divide one of the remaining rectangles equally into three with two vertical pencil lines, and cut out to form the center pieces. Trace around the top and bottom panel, and one center piece, adding ⅝ inch all round for seam allowances, and cut out the pattern pieces.

- For the back, cut a paper pattern 19 x 12⅛ inches.

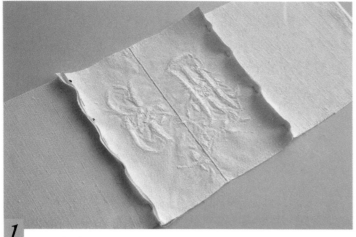

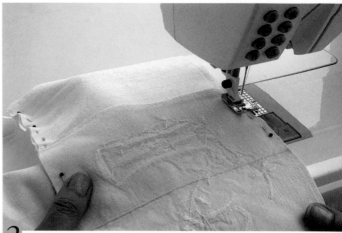

1 From the linen sheet cut out one center piece, placing the monogram in the center. From the remaining linen, cut out two more plain center pieces, two top and bottom panels, and two back pieces, placing one long edge of each back along the deep machine-stitched hem on the sheet. With right sides together and the monogram piece in the center, pin and machine-stitch the three center pieces together. Neaten the seam turnings together with a machine zigzag stitch or a serger. Press the turnings to one side.

2 With right sides together, pin and machine-stitch the long edges of the joined center pieces to the top and bottom panels. Neaten the seam turnings together with a machine zigzag stitch or a serger. Press the turnings to one side.

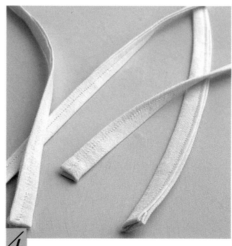

3 Turn the joined front pieces right side up and carefully press the seams flat; pay special attention to the fabric around the monogram.

4 Cut out four tie pieces from the remaining sheet fabric, each one 1½ x 9 inches long and make them up as shown on page 188. Make up the pillow cover as instructed for "The Easiest Pillow," on page 78, following steps 2 to 5, but do not insert the pillow form at this point.

5 Pin a tie to the underside of the top, deep-hemmed back opening edge, placing it 3 inches from the seamed side edge. Pin another tie to the under lapping part of the back to correspond as shown, taking care not to fasten it to the front cover. Repeat with the remaining ties at the other end of the back opening and hand-stitch all the ties in place.

TIPS

- If your monogram is too big to fit into the center panel, adjust the proportions of the pattern pieces accordingly

- Hand-embroidered monograms are very special, and there may be very little fabric to spare around the edges for seam allowances. If this is the case, take a smaller seam turning and double-stitch each seam to strengthen it, making sure you neaten them carefully as given in the instructions.

6 Insert the pillow form through the back opening, smooth the back overlaps out flat, and fasten by tying the ties into bows, as shown.

VARIATIONS

Above: An unusual way to make a central panel is to knit a textured square and insert it into linen side pieces in the same way as for our monogram cushion.

Left: A beautiful piece of embroidery is well worth showing off, whether you stitch it yourself, or buy it ready-made. Let the embroidery speak for itself, and make it up into a simple pillow shape. White and red monograms look wonderful against a natural-colored linen, and red on white is always a classic combination.

Tailored Square Pillow

This is a really versatile pillow style because it looks great in any fabric and can be used in any room of the house. This one features mix-and-match fabrics on the front and back, but you can use just one fabric for a simpler version. The corded edges give a smart appearance.

YOU WILL NEED

- Main decorator fabric for front piece—see right for estimating the yardage

- Contrast decorator fabric for back pieces —see right for estimating the yardage

- Contrast fabric for covering the cable cord—see right for estimating the yardage

- Medium-sized cable cord—enough to fit around the edges of the pillow form, plus 4 inches

- Matching sewing thread

- Ready-made square or rectangular pillow form

- A zipper 4 inches shorter than the finished width of the pillow form

ESTIMATING YARDAGE

- Measure the length and width of the ready-made pillow form.

- For the front, allow one piece of main fabric the size of the form, plus a ⅝-inch seam allowance around all sides.

- For the back, divide the finished form size into two halves. Allow for two pieces of contrast fabric each to this half size, plus a ⅝-inch seam allowance around all sides.

- For covering your cable cord, gauge the width of your fabric strip. To do this, measure around the cord and allow an extra 1¼ inches for seam allowances. Allow for enough straight-grain strips of fabric to fit the length of your cable cord.

PREPARATION

- From the main and contrasting fabrics, cut out the front, back, and cable-cord strip pieces. With right sides facing, pin and baste together the two long edges of the back pieces.

- Machine-stitch 2 inches of the seam together at each end, leaving the center just basted. Press open the seam, and insert the zipper as shown on page 202. Remove all the basting stitches.

1 With right sides together, seam together the contrast cable-cord strips to obtain the length required for covering the cord, and make up the cording as shown on page 186.

2 With the right side up, pin and baste the cording to the outer edges of the top piece, keeping all the raw edges even.

3 At each corner, snip into the cording's seam allowance to help it to bend around the corner. Join the ends of the cording, and stitch it in place, as shown on page 187.

6 Carefully ease out the corners and press the seamed edges flat. Insert the pillow form through the back opening and close the zipper.

4 Lay the corded front right side up. Undo the zipper and lay the back on top of the front, right sides together. Pin and baste the front and back together around the outer edges. Using a zipper foot, and working with the front side, machine-stitch the front and back together. Go over the cording stitch line again, as close to the cording as possible.

5 Remove all basting stitches, clip the seam allowances at the corners, and turn the cover right side out, through the zipper opening.

TIP

If you are using a bulky fabric to make up your cover, it is best to trim away some of the fabric on the seam allowances on each side of the corners, to make it easier to turn them out neatly.

VARIATION

Make corded pillows in any shape or size and pile them together for an informal group. A good tip for coordinating a set of pillows is to use different fabrics from the same range, like these antique-looking linens.

Flanged Pillow

Make a practical flanged pillow cover from a heavyweight striped-cotton fabric. An envelope opening at the back makes it quick and easy to remove for laundering. Use it outdoors on a fine day, to soften the hard corners of a wooden garden seat.

YOU WILL NEED

- Main fabric—see right for estimating yardage

- Matching sewing thread

- Dressmakers' chalk

- Square ready-made pillow form

- Paper for making pattern pieces

- Ruler

ESTIMATING YARDAGE

- Measure the size of your ready-made pillow form.

- For the front pattern piece, draw a square onto paper with the dimensions of the pillow form, and add 2 inches all around for a flanged border, plus ⅝ inch for seam allowances. Cut out the pattern piece.

- For the back pattern piece, fold the front pattern piece in half and draw around the resulting rectangle onto paper. Extend the length of the two short sides by 5½ inches, and draw in a new long side edge to form the overlap for the back envelope opening. Cut out the pattern piece. You will need to allow for two back pattern pieces.

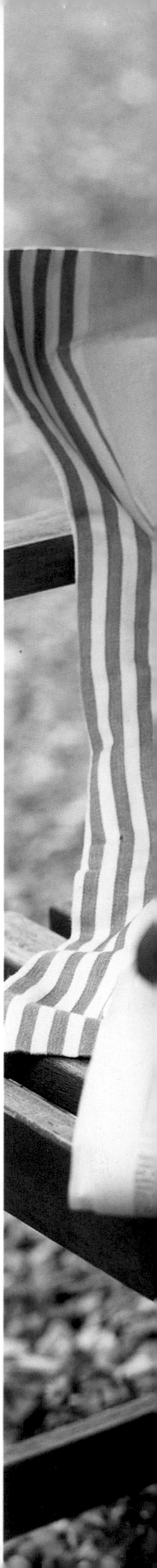

1 From the main fabric, cut out one front pattern piece and two back pattern pieces. Press a double-fold 1¼-inch hem to the wrong side along one long edge of one back piece. Pin and machine-stitch the hem in place. Repeat with the other back piece.

2 With right side up, lay the front piece out on a flat surface. Overlap the hemmed edges of the two back pieces, and place them on top of the front piece, with their wrong sides up and raw edges even. Pin around all the sides with a ⅝-inch seam allowance.

5 Using the dressmakers' chalk and ruler, lightly mark the flanged border 2 inches from the edge, around all sides. Pin and machine-stitch around the cover, using the chalk-line as a guide.

6 To remove the chalk-line, gently rub it with a piece of clean cloth, then insert the pillow form through the back envelope opening.

3 Machine-stitch the front and back pieces together around all edges, removing the pins as you sew.

4 Clip away the excess fabric at the corners, to reduce bulk, then turn the cover through to the right side. Gently use the points of a pair of scissors to ease out the corners, and press the seamed edges flat.

TIP

For a more decorative finish to a flanged edge on a plain fabric pillow cover, try working a second row of machine-stitching ⅜ inch outside the first row, using contrasting colored threads.

VARIATION

Make a smaller flanged border and stitch a length of lace around the edges to make a pretty bed pillow.

Box-Edged Bench Cushions

Take some old box-edged cushions that have seen better days and give them a smart, revamped look with colorful corded-edge covers. A zipper makes the covers easy to remove for laundering.

YOU WILL NEED

- Main decorator fabric—see below for estimating the yardage

- Medium-sized cable cord—see below for estimating the yardage

- Matching sewing thread

- Box-edged cushion form

- A zipper that is 3 inches shorter than the back boxing strip of the cushion form—see estimating the yardage, for size of back boxing strip

- Paper for making the pattern pieces

ESTIMATING YARDAGE

- Measure the length, depth, and width of the box-edged cushion form.

- On the sheet of paper, draw the main panel pattern piece to fit the top and bottom of the cushion form, adding a ⅝-inch seam allowance to all sides. Cut out the pattern piece.

- For the front-and-side boxing strip, draw a strip the depth of the cushion, by the measurement of the front plus the two sides. Subtract 6 inches from the length, then add a ⅝-inch seam all around. Cut out the pattern piece.

- For the back boxing strip, draw a strip half the depth of the cushion by the measurement of the back, plus 6 inches to the length. (This will allow the back boxing strip to extend around the corners.) Add a ⅝-inch seam allowance all around and cut out the pattern piece.

- For the cable cord, you will need enough to go around all of the edges of the top and bottom main panels, plus 4 inches.

- For covering the cable cord, gauge the width of your fabric strip. To do this, measure around the cord and allow an extra 1¼ inches for seam allowances. Allow enough straight-grain strips of fabric to fit the length of your cable cord.

TIP

To make a simpler version, you can omit the zipper. To do this, cut the back boxing strip in one whole piece (the full depth of the cushion form). Make up the cover leaving an opening along the back edge when attaching the bottom panel. Insert the cushion form, and slipstitch the opening edges together by hand.

1 Cut out one top panel, one bottom panel, one front-and-side boxing strip, two back boxing strips, and the cable-cord covering strips. With right sides facing, pin and baste together the two back boxing strips along one long edge.

2 Machine-stitch 1½ inches of the seam together at each end, leaving the center seam basted in place. Press open the seam.

4 With right sides together, pin the short ends of the back boxing strip to the short-ends of the front and side boxing strip, and baste them together with a ⅝-inch seam. Place the joined boxing strip around the cushion form to check that it fits. Adjust it if necessary, then machine-stitch the seams.

5 Make a hand-stitched tailor's tack at the center front and center back of the joined boxing strip. (See page 181.) Mark a corresponding tailor's tack at the center front and back of the top and bottom panel pieces.

3 Insert the zipper into the seam, as shown on page 202.
Remove all the basting stitches.

6 With right sides together, seam together the cable cord strips
to obtain the correct length required for covering the cord,
and make up the cording as shown on page 186. With right
sides up, pin and baste the cording to the outer edges of the
top and bottom panels, keeping raw edges even. At each
corner, snip into the seam allowances of the cording so that
it bends around the corner. Join the ends of the cording and
machine stitch it in place. (See page 187.)

7 With right sides together, pin and baste one edge of the joined
boxing strip around the corded top panel, matching the tailor's
tacks and snipping into the boxing strip seam allowance at
each corner to allow it to bend. Working with the top panel
up, and using the zipper foot on your machine, stitch the
pieces together, re-stitching over the cording stitch line. Make
sure to get as close to the cord as possible.

8 Undo the zipper in the back boxing strip. Pin, baste, and machine-stitch the bottom panel to the remaining raw edge of the boxing strip, as shown in step 7. Remove all the basting stitches.

9 Turn the cover right side out and insert the cushion form through the back opening. Close the zipper.

VARIATIONS

Left: Copy a traditional mattress by stitching circles of fabric on the top and bottom of the cushion, and giving it a quilted effect. Use strong thread and pull the circles up firmly so that the cushion is indented. Remove the circles when washing the cover.

Right: The squab cushion technique can be used in so many ways to update furniture. Here, a wicker bench has been padded with a soft cushion made from floral fabric to create the perfect resting place.

Shaped Box-Edged Cushion

Fit a wooden bench seat with a box-edged cushion that is shaped to fit around the bench seat frame and edged with a smart contrast cording. This type of cushion will also make a comfortable window seat or daybed.

ESTIMATING YARDAGE

- Lay the sheet of paper over the seat of the bench and trace around the edge of the seat, shaping around the frame as necessary. Remove the paper and neaten the drawn lines using a pencil and ruler. Cut out the main seat pattern piece.

- For the front-and-side boxing strip, draw out a strip the depth of the foam by the measurement of the front plus the two sides, incorporating any shaped corners. Take off 6 inches from the total length measurement and add a ⅝-inch seam allowance all around. Cut out the pattern piece.

- For the back boxing strip, draw out a strip to half the depth of the foam by the measurement of the back, plus 6 inches to allow the boxing strip to extend around the corners. Add a ⅝-inch seam allowance all around and cut out the pattern piece.

- Allow enough main fabric for two main seat pieces, one front-and-side boxing strip, and two back boxing strips.

- For the cable cord, you will need to allow enough to go around all the edges of two main seat panels, plus 4 inches.

- For covering the cable cord, first gauge the width of your fabric strip. To do this, measure around the cord and include an extra 1 ¼ inches for seam allowances (See page 186.) Allow enough straight-grain strips of contrast fabric of this width to fit the length of your cable cord.

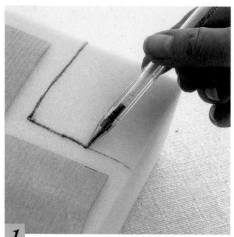

1 Place the main seat pattern piece on top of the foam and draw around it with the fiber-tipped pen. Using a sharp utility or craft knife, cut the foam to size.

2 From the main fabric, cut out two main seat pieces adding a ⅝-inch seam allowance all around, one front-and-side boxing strip, and two back boxing strips (these pieces already have their seam allowances included). From the contrast fabric, cut out the cable-cord covering strips. With right sides together, seam the cable cord strips together to obtain the correct length required for covering the cord. (See page 186.) Make up the cording. (See page 187.) With right sides facing, pin and baste the two back boxing strips together along one long edge.

TIP

As with most seats, this cover will get plenty of wear, so make sure you choose a hardwearing upholstery fabric able to withstand laundering. The contrast cording fabric does not have to be quite as sturdy, but turning the cushion over from time to time will help to spread the wear, keeping your cover looking fresher for longer.

5 Make a hand-stitched tailor's tack at the center front and center back of the joined boxing strip. (See page 181.) Mark a corresponding tailor's tack at the center front and back of both main seat panels.

6 Right sides together, pin and baste one edge of the joined boxing strip around the corded edge of one main seat panel, matching the tailor's tacks, and snipping into the boxing strip seam allowance at each corner to allow it to bend. With the main seat panel uppermost and using a zipper foot, machine-stitch the pieces together, re-stitching over the cording stitch line and as close to the cord as possible.

7 Undo the zipper in the back boxing strip, then pin, baste, and machine-stitch the other main seat panel to the remaining raw edge of the boxing strip, as shown in step 6. Remove all the basting stitches. Turn the cover right side out and press. Insert the foam pad through the back opening and close the zipper.

3 Machine-stitch the basted seam for 1½ inches at each end, leaving the center seam basted in place. Press open the seam. Insert the zipper into the seam, as shown on page 202. Remove the basting stitches. With right sides together, pin the short ends of the back boxing strip to the short ends of the front-and-side boxing strip, and baste them together with a ⅝-inch seam allowance. Place the joined boxing strip around the foam to check that it fits, adjust if necessary, then machine-stitch the seams. Press open the seams.

4 With right sides up, pin and baste the cording to the outer edges of the main seat panels, keeping the raw edges even. At each corner, make a snip into the seam turnings of the cording to help it bend around the corner. Join the ends of the cording, and machine stitch it in place, as shown on page 187.

VARIATION

Make a cover for a child's bench seat with striped blue-and-white ticking. Add color to the room with fresh floral pillows. A low bench like this is ideal for storing baskets of toys underneath.

Tied-On Stool Cover

Once you discover how easy it is to turn up hems with iron-on hemming web, there'll be no stopping you! Try this very simple stool cover for a child's nursery or bedroom. A rectangle of fabric is hemmed all around with iron-on hemming web, placed over the stool seat, and secured at the corners with narrow-ribbon bows. This cover is as easy to replace as it is to make, so have another one ready for when it goes in the laundry.

VARIATION

A more formal look has been achieved with an upholstered cover for a living room ottoman. The fabric has been folded and stapled in place, and matching cording added around the sides.

Tied Neckroll Pillow

This pretty, boudoir neckroll pillow is partly lined with a contrast fabric that picks up the spotted pattern. It is gathered up at both ends with a fabric tie in the contrast fabric to make a softer version of the more tailored bolster pillow shown on page 110.

YOU WILL NEED

- Main fabric—see right for estimating the yardage

- Contrast fabric for lining and ties—see right for estimating the yardage

- Neckroll pillow form

- Matching sewing thread

- Paper for making the pattern pieces

ESTIMATING YARDAGE

- Measure the length, circumference, and diameter of the neckroll pillow form.

- On paper, draw the main pattern piece to the length of the neckroll pillow form plus another 11 inches, by the circumference. Add a ⅝-inch seam allowance to all sides. Cut out the pattern piece.

- For the contrast lining pieces, draw a paper pattern piece that is the circumference measurement by 6 inches deep. Add a ⅝-inch seam allowance to all sides. Cut out the pattern piece.

- Allow for two 2 x 24-inch ties in contrast fabric.

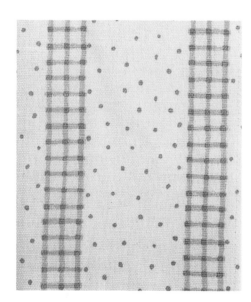

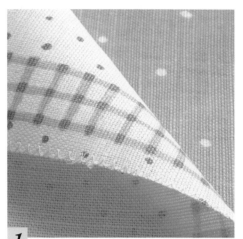

1 From the main fabric, cut out one main piece. From the contrast fabric cut out two lining pieces and two ties. Edge-finish one long side of each lining piece.

2 With right sides together, pin and machine-stitch one short end of the main piece to the corresponding raw edge of one lining piece, taking a ⅝-inch seam allowance. Press the seam open. Repeat at the opposite end with the remaining lining piece.

3 With the right sides together, fold the joined pieces in half, bringing the long edges together and matching up the seams. Machine-stitch the long edges together to form a cylinder.

5 Fold one lining back onto the wrong side of the cylinder, so that the seam sits on the fold. Press along the folded edge. Catch stitch the neatened edge of the lining to the inside of the main fabric to hold it in place. (See page 182.) Repeat with the lining at the opposite end.

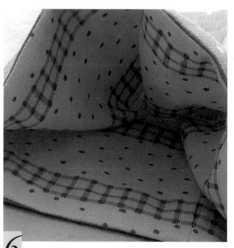

6 Turn the fabric cylinder right side out so the linings are on the inside.

7 Make up two folded ties, with two neatened ends, as shown on page 189.

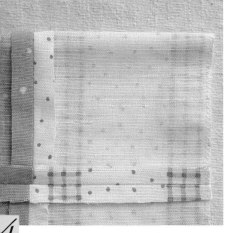

4 Re-fold the cylinder so that the seam runs down the center, and carefully press open the seam allowances.

8 Fold each tie in half and align the fold position with the seam line on the neckroll cover. Pin the ties in place 5¼ inches from both ends and catchstitch them to the seam line. Insert the pillow form into the cover and tie the bows.

TIP

If you wish, use lengths of decorative ribbon or tape to tie the ends of the neckroll pillow instead of making your own ties.

VARIATION

Cover a neckroll pillow quickly and easily without sewing a stitch. Take a lovely old piece of linen with lace trims, and wrap it round the pillow form. Tie the ends firmly with narrow ribbon.

Tailored Bolster Pillow

This stylish bolster pillow, made from a sophisticated mix of striped cotton and silk, is perfect for finishing off the ends of an elegant bench or daybed.

YOU WILL NEED

- Main decorator fabric—see right for estimating the yardage

- Contrast decorator fabric—see right for estimating the yardage

- Contrast fabric for covering the cable cord—see right for estimating the yardage

- Medium-sized cable cord—see right for estimating yardage

- Matching sewing thread

- Bolster pillow form

- A zipper that is 4 inches shorter than the length of the bolster pillow form

- Paper for making the pattern pieces

ESTIMATING YARDAGE

- Measure the length, circumference, and diameter of the bolster pillow form.

- On paper, draw out the main pattern piece to the length of the pillow form by the circumference, and add a ⅝-inch seam allowance to all sides. Cut out the pattern piece.

- For the end pieces, draw a circle to the diameter of the pillow form and add a ⅝-inch seam allowance all around. Cut out the pattern piece.

- For the cable cord, allow twice the circumference plus 4 inches.

- For covering your cable cord, first gauge the width of your fabric strip. To do this, measure around the cord and include an extra 1¼ inches for seam allowances. Allow for enough straight-grain strips of fabric of this width to fit the length of your cable cord.

1 From the main and contrasting fabrics, cut out one main pattern piece, two ends, and the cable cord strip pieces. Work a row of machine stay stitching ⅜ inch from the circumference edges of the main piece. (See page 183.) Clip into the seam allowances at regular intervals, no closer than ⅛ inch to the stitch line.

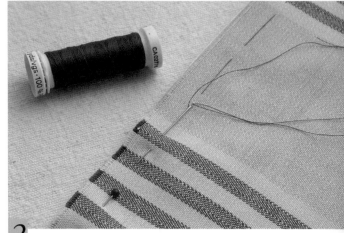

2 With right sides together, fold the main fabric piece in half, bringing its unclipped edges together to make a cylinder. Pin and baste the edges together with a ⅝-inch seam allowance.

4 Make up the cording as shown on page 186. Clip into the seam turnings at regular intervals, getting no closer than ⅛ inch to the stitch line, to help the cording fit around the curves of the cushion ends.

5 Cut the cording into two equal lengths. Pin and baste a length onto the right side of each circular end piece. Join the ends of the cording and stitch in place, as shown on page 187.

TIPS

- For an alternative to making your own cording, hand stitch decorative drapery cord around the ends of the bolster after the pillow cover has been completed.

- If you have difficulty machine-stitching the zipper into the fabric cylinder, stitch as far as the center from one end, then remove from the machine, turn the cylinder around, and stitch toward the center from the other end.

3 Machine-stitch a 2-inch long seam at both ends, leaving the center seam basted in place. Press open the seam and insert the zipper as shown on page 202. Remove all basting stitches.

6 Undo the zipper in the main piece, and with right sides together, pin the corded end pieces to the clipped ends of the main piece. Pin and baste them in place. Using a zipper foot on your machine, and working with the end pieces on top, stitch the pieces together, restitching over the cording stitches, as close to the cording as possible. Remove the basting stitches and turn the cover to the right side. Insert the pillow form through the opening and close the zipper.

VARIATION

Pleat the ends into a neat circle for a slightly less formal bolster cushion. It only takes one length of fabric with a single seam down the side. A striped fabric makes a feature of the circular end piece and can be finished off with a jaunty tassel at either end.

Beanbag Chair

A comfortable, squashy seat made from lightweight polystyrene pellets inside an inner muslin shell. The gorgeous outer slipcover is made from striped silk with a faux-suede top. Children will love to bounce and sink into this seat, but its sophisticated fabrics make it smart enough to grace any living room too.

YOU WILL NEED

- Main decorator fabric for the sides—see right for estimating the yardage

- Contrast decorator fabric for the top and base—see right for estimating the yardage.

- Muslin fabric—the same quantity as the main and contrast fabrics together

- Matching sewing thread

- A zipper 3 inches shorter than the diameter of the base

- Polystyrene pellets

- Pencil

- Parcel twine

- Plastic push pin or brass drawing pin

- Paper for making a pattern

ESTIMATING YARDAGE

- Decide on the diameter (width) and height of your beanbag chair.

- Cut out a square of paper about 2 inches larger than the diameter you want for the top. Fold the paper in half, and half again, making four equal quarters. Cut a length of the twine that is 8 inches longer than one of the folded edges. Tie one end of the twine to the pencil, and attach the other end to the folded corner of the paper with the push pin or drawing pin. Making sure the twine is now exactly half the length of your diameter (radius), and keeping the twine taut, draw an arc from one edge of the paper to the other using the pencil. Carefully cut out the pattern along the curved line, through all layers of paper, and open the pattern out to create a full circle. (See steps 1, 2, 3, 4, and 5 on pages 148–149.) You will need to allow for one top piece from contrast fabric, plus a ⅝-inch seam allowance all around.

- For the base, fold the top pattern in half. You will need to allow for two base pieces from contrast fabric, plus a ⅝-inch seam allowance all around.

- For the sides, measure around the circumference of the top pattern piece, and allow for a rectangle of main fabric the circumference measurement, plus 1¼ inches for seam allowances, by the finished height, plus 1¼ inches for seam allowances.

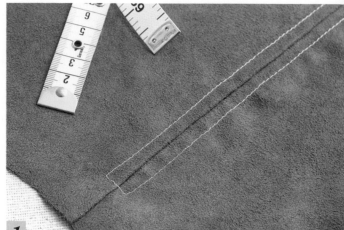

1 From the main fabric, cut out one side piece; from the contrast fabric, one top and two base pieces; from the muslin, one top, one side and two base pieces. With right sides together, pin and baste the straight edges of the base pieces, with a ⅝-inch seam allowance. Machine-stitch the seam together, for 1½ inches at either end, leaving the center just basted. Press the seam open, and insert the zipper as shown on page 202. Remove all the basting stitches.

4 With right sides together, match the base zipper seam to the side seam, and the other end of the zipper seam and tailor's tacks to the side piece tailor's tacks.

5 Pin the pieces together all around, placing the pins at right angles to the seam, and easing the fabric between pins. Baste and machine-stitch the pieces together, with a ⅝-inch seam allowance.

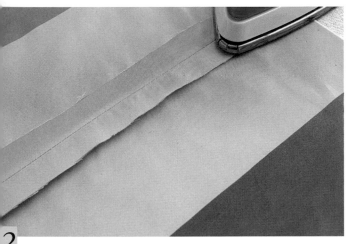 

2 With right sides facing, fold the side piece in half, bringing the two short edges together. Pin and machine-stitch the short edges together with a ⅝-inch seam allowance to form a ring. Press open the seam.

3 Matching the seams, fold the base piece in half across the zipper, and work a hand-sewn tailor's tack (see page 181) to mark the fold at each side. Lay the seamed side piece on a flat surface with the seam running down one edge. Mark the opposite fold with hand-sewn tailor's tack on the bottom edge. Refold the side, lining the tailor's tack up with the seam, and mark the two new folds, as before.

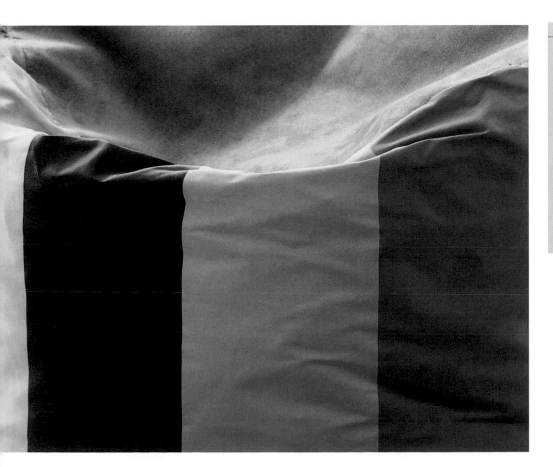

TIP

You can re-cover a ready-made beanbag in the same way. Just measure your old beanbag to find out the dimensions to cut out your new slipcover.

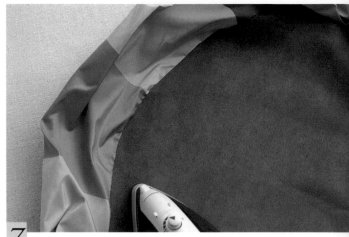

6 Work four tailor's tacks on the top piece and three on the top edge of the side piece to mark the quarter positions, as before. Open up the zipper. With right sides facing, and tailor's tacks and seams matching, pin, baste, and machine-stitch the top to the sides, as shown for the base.

7 Turn the cover through to the right side, and press. Make the inner shell as shown for the main cover, but omit the zipper. Fill the shell with the polystyrene pellets through the zipper opening until it is about three-quarters full. Firmly slipstitch the zipper opening edges. (See page 183.) Push the inner muslin beanbag inside the outer cover through the zipper opening, lining up the top and base panels, and close the zipper.

VARIATIONS

Left: A cylindrical piece of high-density, flame-retardant foam can be covered in the same way as the beanbag chair to make a comfortable seat for outdoors or a footstool for the living room.

Right: Make a set of extra large pillows, fill with polystyrene pellets, and use them as floor cushions. If you have bare, sanded floors, they will be welcomed as a comfortable place to lounge and play games.

BEDROOM FURNISHINGS

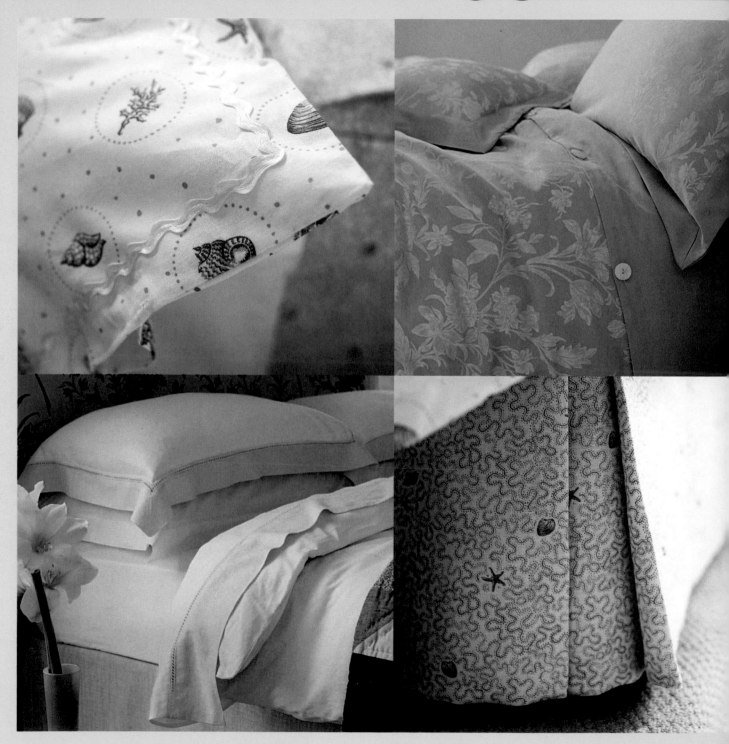

Duvet Cover

Making your own duvet cover means that you can coordinate the bed with the rest of the room scheme. Use a good-quality cotton fabric that is suitable for frequent laundering, and trim it with a simple rickrack braid. The two sides of this duvet cover have been made in different colorways of the same fabric, allowing you to make a change with ease.

YOU WILL NEED

- Main fabric for the top—see right for estimating the yardage

- Contrast fabric for the back—see right for estimating the yardage

- Matching sewing thread

- A length of snap tape—see right for estimating the yardage

- Rickrack braid—see right for estimating the yardage

- Dressmakers' chalk

- Ruler

TIP

Use cotton or polyester/cotton sheeting if you want to avoid joining fabric widths for your duvet cover. This is available in much wider widths than conventional decorator fabrics, although the choice of colors and patterns are limited.

ESTIMATING YARDAGE

- Measure the length and width of your duvet.

- For the front and back panels, add 2³⁄₈ inches to the length measurement for hems and seam allowances, and 1¼ inches to the width for seam allowances. You may need to join fabric widths to obtain your correct fabric size. Always place full panels at the center with part panels at each side.

- You will need enough snap tape to fit the width of the duvet, minus 4 inches.

- For the rickrack braid, allow enough to go around the outer edges of your duvet.

1 Join the fabric widths, if necessary, with French seams matching any patterns to form the correct size. (See page 185.) Cut out one top panel from the main fabric and one backing panel from the contrast. Press a double-fold 1-inch hem onto the wrong side along the lower edge of both the top and back panels.

2 Fold the back panel in half lengthways to find the center. Make a tailor's tack on the hem to mark the fold. (See page 181.) Mark the central point on each side of the snap tape with a pin; separate the two sides. Open the back panel and pin one tape along the hem on the right side. Make sure snaps face the correct way and that the pin and tailor's tack are aligned.

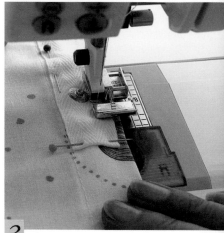

3 Repeat step 2 with the top panel, using the other side of the snap tape, and making sure the snaps still line up, when the central markers are matched. Using a zipper foot on your machine, stitch the pieces of tape to the front and back panels around all the edges of the tape.

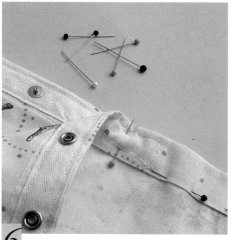

6 With right sides facing, fasten the snap tape, and pin the top and back panels together along the lower edge. Pin across the tape ends at right angles to the bottom edge and along the machined hemlines to the raw side edges. Machine-stitch along the pin-lines through all layers of fabric and tape.

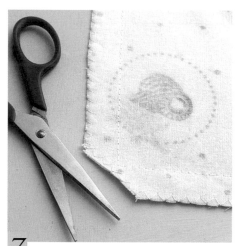

7 Pin the top and back panels together around the remaining three raw-sides, and machine-stitch them together. Neaten the seam allowances with a machine zigzag stitch or use a serger. Clip across the seam allowances at the top two corners.

8 Open up the snap tape and turn the cover right side out. Carefully push out the corners, and press the seamed edges flat. Insert the duvet through the opening and close the snaps.

4 Using the dressmakers' chalk and a ruler, lightly draw a border on the top panel, 2½ inches from the top and side raw edges, and 2 inches from the bottom inner tape edge.

5 Pin the rickrack braid around the chalked line, and machine-stitch in place, sewing along the center of the braid.

VARIATION

Once you have made a simple duvet cover, you can add all sorts of decorative finishes. Here, two fabrics, one used as a plain wide border, and the other in a subtle floral design, are buttoned together. With coordinating pillows, the set makes a smart, contemporary look.

125

Self-Bordered Sham Cover

Transform your pillows with a flat self-bordered sham cover to match your duvet and create a pretty coordinated set that will enhance your bedroom. Choose a cotton fabric that's suitable for frequent laundering.

YOU WILL NEED

- Main fabric—see right for estimating the yardage

- Rickrack braid—see right for estimating the yardage

- Matching sewing thread

- Dressmakers' chalk

- Ruler

ESTIMATING YARDAGE

- Measure the length and width of your pillow sham.

- For the top, or front panel, you will need one piece measuring the width by the length, plus 2⅝ inches around for the self-border, and seam allowances.

- For the bottom, or back panel, you will need one piece measuring the width by the length. Add 5¼ inches to the width measurement for the self-border and seam allowances, and 4 inches to the length for the border, hem, and seam allowances.

- For the back flap, you will need one piece measuring the width, plus 5¼ inches for the self-border and seam allowances, by 10½ inches deep.

- For the rickrack braid, allow enough to go around the outer edges of your pillow sham, plus 4 inches.

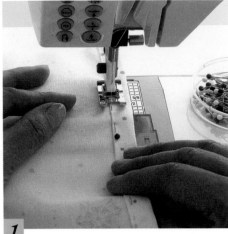

1 Cut out one front, one back, and one back flap panel. Press a double-fold ½-inch hem onto the wrong side along one long edge of the back flap. Pin and machine-stitch in place.

2 Press a ⅜-inch hem onto the wrong side along one short edge of the back panel, then press over another 1½-inch hem. Pin and machine-stitch in place.

3 With right sides facing, seam the long-raw edge of the back flap, to one short edge of the front panel. Seam the remaining short-raw edge of the back panel to the remaining short-raw edge of the front panel. Finish the seams with a machine zigzag stitch, or use a serger.

5 Finish the seams with a machine zigzag stitch, or use a serger, if you own one. Clip across the seam turnings at the corners.

6 Turn the cover to the right side and carefully push out the corners. Press the seamed edges flat.

7 Using the dressmakers' chalk and ruler lightly draw a border 2 inches from all edges.

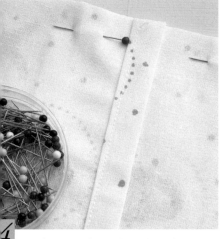

4 Lay the joined panels, right side up, on a flat surface. Fold the back panel over the front panel along the seam line. Next fold the back flap over the front panel, overlapping the back panel, too. Pin and machine-stitch the pieces together along the raw side edges, with a ⅝-inch seam allowance.

VARIATION

Contrasting edges give these pillows a fresh, crisp look that sits well with the figured wallpaper behind the bed and the clean lines of the window. The edges can be stitched in strips before the pillowcase is made up.

8 Pin and machine-stitch around the chalked-line to form the border.

9 Pin the rickrack braid to the front of the cover around the stitched line, and machine-stitch the braid in place, through all layers of fabric. Insert the pillow sham through and under the back flap.

TIP

The same fabric has been used here to make both the front and back of the sham cover, but you can use a contrasting color for the back pieces, as shown for the duvet cover on page 122.

Pleated Dust Ruffle

Hide a plain bed base behind a fitted dust ruffle, neatly concealing any under-bed clutter or storage. Made in sections, the dust ruffle has overlapping flaps that look like box pleats and that make it easy to pull out drawers or boxes. Choose a fabric to coordinate with your bedding; here the dainty pink-and-white cotton fabric with a tiny shell design ties in perfectly with the larger design on the duvet. (See pages 122–125.)

YOU WILL NEED

- Main fabric—see right for estimating the yardage

- Plain cotton sheeting fabric—see right for estimating the yardage

- Drapery lining—see right for estimating the yardage

- Matching sewing thread

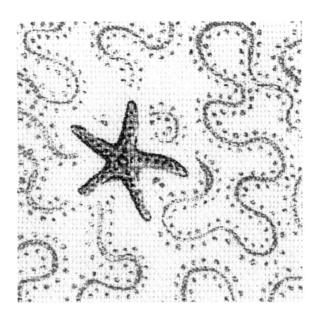

ESTIMATING YARDAGE

- To find the size of the top piece, measure the width and length of the bed base (without the mattress), and add ⅝ inch all around for seam and hem allowances. Allow one piece of plain sheeting to the measurements calculated.

- To find the depth of the side- and end-panels, measure the height of the bed base from the top to the floor (without the mattress), and add 1½ inches to the measurement for seam and hem allowances.

- Each side of the bed is divided into two separate panels for ease of access under the bed. For each of the four side-panels allow a main fabric piece half the length of the bed, plus 7 inches for the pleats and 1¼ inches for seam allowances, by the depth calculated.

- For one end-panel, allow a piece of main fabric the width of the bed, plus 7 inches for the pleats and 1¼ inches for seam allowances, by the depth calculated.

- For the pleat backings, allow four pieces of main fabric 8¼ inches, by the depth calculated.

- For the lining, allow for four side-panels, one end-panel, and four pleat backings to the same width as the main fabric, but ¾ inch shorter.

1 From the main fabric and lining, cut out the side and end panels and the pleat backings. From the plain sheeting fabric, cut out one top piece. Finish the top edge (head) of the top piece with machine zigzag stitch, or use a serger, and then press the edge ⅝ inch onto the wrong side. Pin and machine-stitch the hem in place.

2 With right sides facing, and raw edges even, lay a lining side-panel piece on top of a main fabric side-panel piece. Pin and machine-stitch the pieces together with a ⅝-inch seam allowance along the lower edge. Press the seam toward the lining.

5 Trim the corners and turn the panel right side out. Press the seamed edges flat.

6 Along both side edges, press 3½ inches onto the wrong side to form the front of the pleat. Pin the pleats in place along the top edge. Repeat steps 2, 3, 4, 5, and 6 with the remaining side panels, the end panel, and pleat backing pieces.

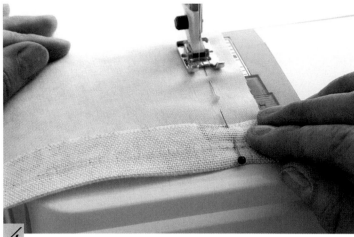

3 With right sides facing, fold the lining on top of the main fabric matching the raw edges at the top and sides. Very lightly press the folded edge so that a strip of main fabric shows along the bottom edge of the lining.

4 Making sure the top edges of the fabric and lining are even, pin and machine-stitch a ⅝-inch seam down both short sides of the panel.

7 Fold the plain top piece in half, bringing the finished top edge to lie ⅝ inch from the raw lower edge and mark the fold at both side edges with pins. Open the top panel out flat and with right sides facing and raw edges even, place two side panels along one side edge of the top piece, matching the pressed pleat edges together at the center pin position. Pin the side panels in place.

8 At the back edge of the top piece, the pressed pleat edges of the side-panels should finish ⅝ inch in from the raw edge. Pin and machine-stitch the side panels to the top piece with a ⅝-inch seam allowance. Repeat with other two side panels on the remaining side edge of the top piece.

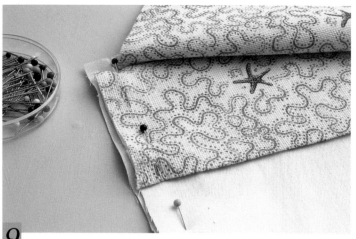

9 At the top back edge, fold the side panels back out of the way, and with right sides together, pin the raw edge of the end panel to the top piece. The pressed pleat edges should sit ⅝ inch from the sides. Pin and machine-stitch the end-panel in place with a ⅝-inch seam allowance. Fold the side-panels back over the end panel.

10 Fold one pleat backing in half, and mark the center of the top raw edge with a hand-sewn tailor's tack. (See page 181.) With wrong sides uppermost and raw edges even, lay the pleat backing over the pressed pleat of a side-panel, matching the tailor's tack to the corner, ⅝ inch from the base edge. Pin and machine-stitch the pleat backing in place, through all layers of fabric, ending at the tailor's tack.

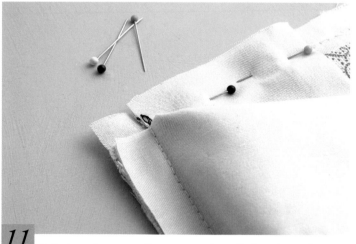

11 Snip into the seam allowance at the tailor's tack to allow the pleat backing to turn the corner. Pin and machine-stitch the remaining top edge of pleat backing in place along the base panel. Repeat steps 10 and 11 for the opposite base corner.

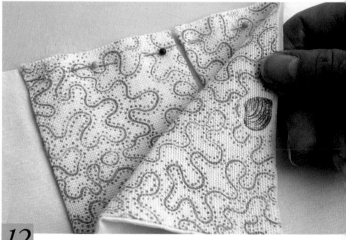

12 Mark the center of another pleat backing with a tailor's tack and, with wrong sides up, lay it over the central pressed pleats of the two side-panels, matching the tailor's tack to the center. Pin and machine-stitch the pleat backing in place. Repeat for the opposite side. Turn the finished dust ruffle to the right side and press. Place it over the bed base, and then replace the mattress.

VARIATION

Many divan beds have a base that you don't want to look at every day. For a fixed base without drawers, make a dust ruffle with an inverted pleat in each corner. (See page 190.) Pull it over the top to make a tailored cover that coordinates with your bedroom. Make two narrow ties and tie into a bow at the corners to complete the look.

TIP

To ensure that the side and base panels will fit correctly, fold and temporarily pin the pleats in place. Then try them against the top piece for size. Adjust the pleat depths, if necessary, before pressing and stitching them permanently in place.

Headboard Cover

Create a beautiful sanctuary, where you can relax at the end of the day, by making a custom headboard for your bed. See pages 200–201 for how to make and pad your own headboard, and then sew a smart, fitted cover to coordinate with your curtains and dust ruffle.

YOU WILL NEED

- Main decorator fabric—see right for estimating the yardage

- Medium-sized cable cord—see right for estimating yardage

- Matching sewing thread

- Hook-and-loop tape—see right for calculating yardage

- Headboard. (See pages 200–201 for instructions on how to make your own.)

ESTIMATING YARDAGE

- With the headboard fastened to the bed or with the bed base pushed up to the headboard, measure the height from the top to 4 inches above the bed base, and measure the width. Allow for two panels of fabric the height measurement by the width measurement, plus a ⅝-inch seam allowance all around. You may have to join fabric widths to obtain your correct panel width.

- For the cable cord, you will need to allow enough to go up the two sides of the main panel and across the top, plus 4 inches.

- For covering the cable cord, first gauge the width of your fabric strip. To do this, measure around the cord and allow an extra 1¼ inches for seam allowances. (See page 186.) Allow enough bias-grain strips of contrast fabric, of this width, to fit the length of your cable cord.

- You will need enough hook-and-loop tape to fit down one side edge of the headboard, less 4 inches.

1 From the main fabric, cut out two pieces for the front and back panels and the bias cable-cord covering strips. Join any fabric widths, if necessary, to obtain the correct panel widths. (See page 184). With right sides together, seam the cable-cord strips together to obtain the correct length required for covering the cord, and make up the cording as shown on page 186.

2 With right sides up, pin and baste the cording to the outer edges of the front panel, keeping raw edges even. To help the cording round the corners, snip into the cording seam allowance, as shown.

3 To finish the ends, trim the cording level with the bottom edge of the front panel. Undo about 2 inches of the cording stitching; trim away ⅝ inch of the uncovered cable cord and fold the covering strip back over to neaten, as shown. Pin in place.

6 Using a zipper foot on your machine, stitch the back panel to the front panel along the pinned edges, re-stitching over the cording stitch line and making sure you get as close to the cord as possible. Snip into the seam allowance around the corners. Finish the bottom raw edges of both the front and back panels with a machine zigzag stitch, or use a serger.

7 Turn the cover to the right side; push out the corners; and press the cover flat.

8 Open the two sides of the hook-and-loop tape and pin the loop section to the wrong side of the opening on the front panel, butting the edge of the tape against the cording. Machine-stitch the tape in place around all edges of the tape. Repeat on the other edge of the opening, stitching the hook side of the tape to the right side of the back panel.

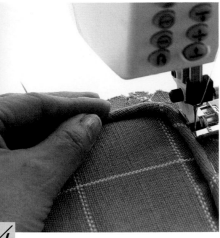

4 Using a zipper foot on your machine, stitch the cording to the front panel, stitching as close to the cord as possible.

5 With right sides together, place the back panel on top of the front, sandwiching the cording in-between. Pin the pieces together up one side, across the top and down the opposite side for 4 inches only.

VARIATION

A shaped headboard is just as easy to cover if you trace the shape onto paper to make a pattern for the fabric. Vary the fastenings, too—instead of hook-and-loop tape, make long ties for the sides to hold it in place.

9 Pull the cover over the headboard and smooth it down until it fits snugly. Press the two sections of the hook-and-loop tape together to close the opening edge. Push the mattress up to the headboard to conceal the lower edge if it is not fixed to the bed base.

Bedroom Stool Cover

Transform a stool for the bedroom with a simple inverted-pleat cover that is both elegant and stylish, and gives a plain piece of furniture a new look. Choose a pretty decorator fabric that is tough enough to withstand the wear-and-tear of constant use, and add four pressed pleats to the long skirt. It is the perfect addition to a traditional style bedroom.

YOU WILL NEED

- Main decorator fabric—see right for estimating the yardage

- Matching sewing thread

- Paper for making a pattern

ESTIMATING YARDAGE

- For the top, or seat piece, place the sheet of paper on top of the stool and trace around the edge to make a pattern. Add a ⅝-inch seam allowance. Then cut out the shape, making sure that the edges of the shape form smooth curves. Allow enough fabric for one top piece.

- For the skirt piece, measure the circumference of the seat and add 10 inches for each of the four pleats, plus 1¼ inches for seam allowances.

- Measure the height of the stool from the top of the seat to the floor and add 1⅝ inches for the lower hem and top seam allowance. Allow for a piece of fabric that is the calculated circumference, by the height. You may need to join fabric pieces to get the required size.

1 Cut out the top and skirt pieces from the fabric, and join any fabric widths, if necessary, to obtain your correct circumference length. (See page 184.) With right sides facing fold the skirt in half, bringing the two short straight edges together. Pin, baste, and machine-stitch the edges together taking a ⅝-inch seam allowance. Press open the seam allowances.

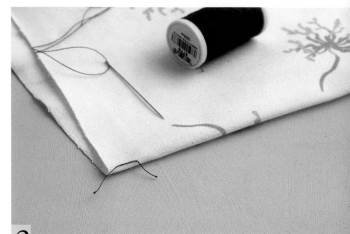

2 Fold the skirt piece into four equal quarters, and mark the pleat positions at the quarter folds with hand-sewn tailor's tacks at both the top and bottom skirt edges. (See page 181.)

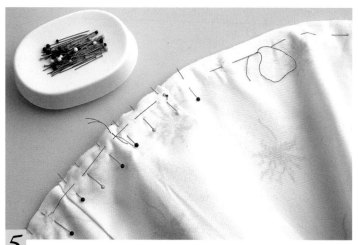

5 With right sides together, pin the skirt to the top piece, matching up the tailor's tacks. Place the pins at right angles to the seam, easing the fabric between the pins. Baste and machine-stitch the pieces together with a ⅝-inch seam allowance. Remove the pins and basting stitches.

6 Finish the seams with a machine zigzag stitch, or use a serger. Turn the cover to the right side and press.

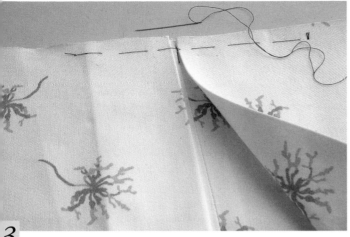

3 Fold and press a 5-inch-wide inverted pleat at each marked pleat position, placing the tailor's tack at the center of each pleat. (See page 190.) Pin and baste the pleats in place at the top edge.

4 Fold the shaped top piece into four equal quarters, and mark the folds with hand-sewn tailor's tacks at the edge, as before.

7 Press a double-fold ½-inch hem to the wrong side along the bottom edge of the skirt piece. Pin and machine-stitch the hem in place. Give the cover a final press, paying special attention to the pleats, and place it over the stool.

TIP

If you need to join the fabric pieces to obtain the correct skirt size, try to join the fabric inside the pleats, preferably with the seam running along the inner fold of the pleat so that it does not show from the right side.

VARIATION

Instead of making inverted pleats, gather the skirt piece to fit the top piece for a softer, country-style cover.

ACCESSORIES

Circular Tablecloth

This easy-to-make round tablecloth can be sewn in just a couple of hours. Use it over a fiberboard table to hide a plain surface. You will be left with remnants after cutting out the circular shape from the fabric. Cut these into large squares and hem the edges to make a set of matching napkins.

YOU WILL NEED

- Fabric—see right for estimating the yardage

- Matching sewing thread

- A large sheet of paper for making a pattern

- Pencil

- Parcel twine

- Plastic push pin or brass drawing pin

ESTIMATING YARDAGE

- Take the measurement from the center of your tabletop to the floor, or the desired tablecloth length, and add ⅜ inch for a hem allowance.

- To estimate your fabric quantity, double this measurement to find the finished size of your tablecloth and allow for a square of fabric this size.

1 Cut out a square of fabric to the required measurements. Fold the fabric in half, and then again into quarters.

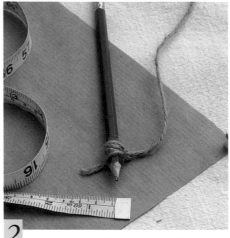

2 Cut a square of paper that is slightly larger than the folded fabric and a length of the twine that is 8 inches longer than one of the folded edges. Tie one end of the twine to the pencil and attach the other end to the corner of the paper with the push pin.

3 Make sure the twine is now exactly the same length as one folded edge of the fabric. On a large flat surface, and keeping the twine taut, draw an arc from one edge of the paper to the other using the pencil. Cut out the paper pattern along the curved line.

4 Place the paper pattern on the folded fabric, with the straight edges along the fold lines and the center points matching. Pin the pattern in place, and cut along the curved edge through all thicknesses of fabric.

5 Remove the pattern and open out the fabric to form the complete circle.

6 Work a row of stay stitching in matching thread all around the edge of the cloth ⅜ inch from the edge. (See page 183.) Finish the edges with either a machine zigzag stitch, or use a serger. Press the neatened edges flat. (A contrast-colored thread has been used in these photos simply to make them easier to follow.)

TIP

You may need to join fabric widths to get the right size. If so, position a full width in the center and add a half width on either side, joining the fabric with a French seam. (See page 185.)

7 Press a ⅜-inch hem onto the wrong side, making sure the stay-stitching row is just inside the hem turning. Pin and machine-stitch the hem in place all around the edge.

VARIATION

A small round table in a tiny kitchen only needs a cloth thrown over to turn it into a welcoming place for breakfast. A square cloth looks less formal than a round one, and is very quick to make. Just hem around the four edges and it's ready.

Weighted Tablecloth

Don't let summer breezes spoil your enjoyment when eating outdoors—make a tablecloth with little corner pockets that hold lead weights. On a windy day, the cloth will stay securely in place rather than billowing in the air. These small weights, which look like flat buttons, are designed to be slipped into the hems of curtains and drapery, and can be purchased wherever drapery hardware is sold.

YOU WILL NEED

- Fabric—see right for estimating the yardage

- Matching sewing thread

- Four curtain weights

- A sheet of paper for making a pattern

- Ruler

- Triangle, or similar right-angled object

ESTIMATING YARDAGE

- Measure the length and width of the tabletop and decide on the depth of the overhang at the sides.

- Add twice the overhang depth to both the length and width measurements, plus a 1¼-inch hem allowance for all sides.

1 Cut out the fabric. Press a ⅝-inch double-fold hem onto the wrong side all around; pin; and machine-stitch in place.

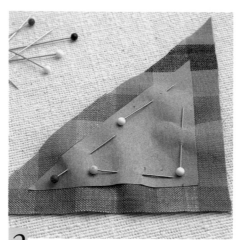

2 Using the ruler and triangle, draw a right-angled triangle on the paper, making the two straight lines 3 inches long. Cut out the pattern, then pin it onto a piece of the remaining fabric. Leaving a ⅜-inch hem allowance all around, cut out four triangles of fabric.

3 Press a ⅜-inch single-turned hem onto the wrong side all around, trimming the excess fabric at the corners.

4 With wrong sides facing, place one triangular piece over one corner of the tablecloth, with straight side edges level. Pin and machine-stitch in place close to the edge, along the two straight sides only.

5 Slip a curtain weight into the triangular pocket at the corner, through the open diagonal side.

6 Pin and machine-stitch close to the edge, across the diagonal side to enclose the weight. Repeat steps 4, 5, and 6 with the remaining tablecloth corners, fabric triangles, and weights.

TIP

If your table is large, you may need to join fabric widths to get the right size. If so, position a full width in the center, and add a half width either side, joining the fabric with a French seam. (See page 185.)

Ruched Lampshade

Dressy and feminine, a ruched fabric lampshade makes the perfect complement to a hand-carved and gilded lamp base in a traditional setting. You can even make one to transform the most ordinary lampbase into something special.

YOU WILL NEED

- Main decorator fabric—see right for estimating the yardage

- Drapery lining fabric—see right for estimating the yardage

- Matching sewing thread

- 1 yard of ⅜-inch-wide cotton tape

- 1 yard of ⅜-inch-wide velvet ribbon

- Bodkin or large safety pin

- Seam ripper

- A wire lampshade frame or a plain lampshade

ESTIMATING YARDAGE

- Measure the height of the lampshade frame and add 6 inches to the measurement for an overhang and hems.

- For the width, measure all around the base of the frame and double the measurement.

- Allow for a piece of main fabric that is the height, by the width calculated.

- For the lining, allow for a piece the same size as the main fabric, but subtract 1¼ inches from the height measurement.

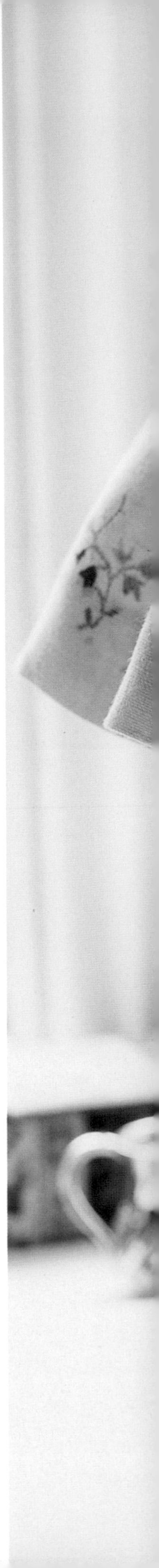

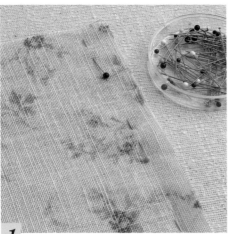

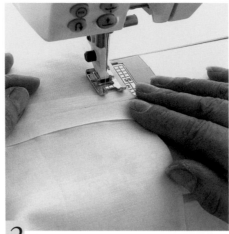

1 From the main fabric and lining, cut out the lampshade pieces. Join any fabric pieces, if necessary, to obtain the correct widths. (See page 184.) With right sides facing, pin and machine-stitch the short ends of the main fabric together to form a ring. Press open the seam. Repeat with the lining.

2 With right sides together, place the fabric ring inside the lining ring, keeping the bottom edges even and side seams matching. Pin and machine-stitch the pieces together around the bottom edges with a ⅝-inch seam allowance.

3 Open out the pieces and, working from the wrong side, press the bottom edge seam allowance up toward the lining.

5 Press a 2-inch hem onto the wrong side along the top edge of the main fabric and a 1¼-inch hem onto the wrong side along the top edge of the lining.

6 Pin the pressed top edge of the lining onto the main fabric all around, then pin another line ⅜ inch down from the top row of pins. Machine-stitch along both lines of pins to form a casing.

7 Using the seam ripper, carefully open the seam in the lining between the two rows of machine stitching.

TIP

The color of the lining you choose will affect the glow your lamp gives. Pale pink silk will give a wonderful rosy glow to the room, but experiment with different color samples by draping them over a lit shade.

VARIATION

Reuse a well-laundered vintage linen tea towel when you gather it into a lampshade. The strong fabric and slightly faded red stripe is just right for a kitchen, giving it a utilitarian look that balances the frills.

4 With wrong sides facing, fold the lining back over the main fabric so that a 1½ inch-wide strip of main fabric shows along the lower edge of the lining. Press the folded bottom edge flat.

8 Thread the cotton tape into the bodkin or attach the safety pin to one end. Thread the tape through the casing and back out, leaving approximately 4 inches showing at each end.

9 Pull up the tape so that the shade cover gathers to fit the top of the lampshade, then tie the tape ends together.

10 Turn the cover to the right side and adjust the gathers. Place the cover over the lampshade frame. Wrap the velvet ribbon around the ruched top casing and tie the ends into a decorative bow.

Lined Wicker Trunk

Transform a wicker trunk with a pretty cotton lining that simply slips inside, and stays in place with ties around the hinges. This practical lining keeps the dust from entering through the woven wicker-work, making the trunk ideal for storing linen in a bedroom or spare pillows and throws in a living room.

YOU WILL NEED

- Main fabric—see right for estimating the yardage
- 1 yard of ⅜-inch-wide cotton tape
- Matching sewing thread
- Contrast-colored sewing thread

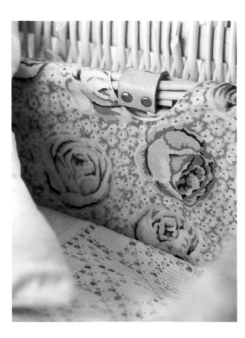

ESTIMATING YARDAGE

- For the bottom piece, measure the length and width of the trunk base, on the inside, and allow for a rectangle of fabric to these measurements, plus a ⅝-inch seam allowance all around.

- For the side pieces, measure the depth of the trunk on the inside, from the top to the base. Allow for a rectangle of fabric the depth of the trunk, plus 5 inches for an overhang, casing, and seam allowance, by twice the length and width measurements, plus 1¼ inches for seam allowances.

- For the main tie, measure around the top edge of the trunk, from the outside edge of one back hinge, around the front, sides, and back to the outside edge of the opposite back hinge, and add 24 inches to the measurement. Allow for a 2-inch-wide straight-grain strip of fabric, by the length calculated.

- For the back tie, measure the distance between the inner edges of the two back hinges, and add 24 inches to the measurement. Allow for a 2-inch-wide straight-grain strip of fabric, by the length calculated.

1 Cut out one base and one side piece. Cut out the tie strips, joining them if necessary to obtain the correct lengths. With right sides facing, fold the side piece in half, bringing the short edges together, and seam the edges together with a ⅝-inch seam allowance. Press open the seam allowances.

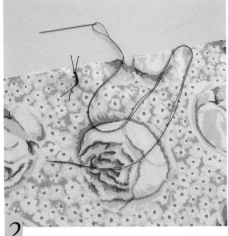

2 Fold the base piece in half lengthwise, and mark the center folds with hand-sewn tailor's tacks. (See page 181.)

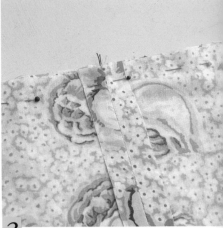

3 Lay out the joined side piece with the seam allowance running down one edge. Mark the opposite fold with a tailor's tack, close to the edge. With right sides facing and raw edges even, pin the sides to the base around all edges, lining up the seam to one base tailor's tack and with remaining tacks matching. Machine-stitch in place with a ⅝-inch seam allowance.

4 Clip into the side seam allowance, cutting no closer than ⅛ inch from the stitching, at each corner. This will help to turn the corners, as shown.

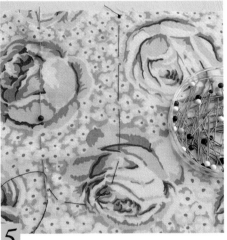

5 Fit the lining into the trunk, with the wrong sides of the fabric facing the wicker, and push it down neatly into the corners. Using pins, mark a scooped shape around the hinges at the back top edge of the lining, as shown. Remove the lining from the trunk.

TIP

Instead of using a cotton tape to neaten the edges of the scooped out hinge sections, make or buy some ready-made folded bias binding. This can be stitched in place and carefully stretched around the outer edge, eliminating the need to clip into the tape in order to help it lay flat around the curves.

VARIATION

A small basket on wheels can be used as a moveable toy chest or turned into a cute bed for dolls and teddies. Here, it's trimmed with a removable lining in blue-and-white checked cotton.

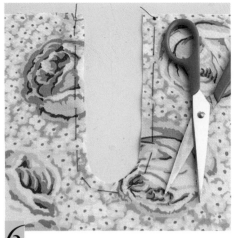

6 Baste around the pin lines with a contrasting colored thread and remove the pins. Cut around the scooped shape, just inside the line, leaving a ¼ inch for seam allowances.

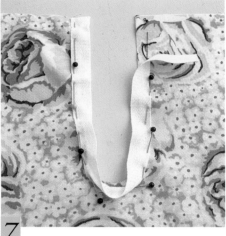

7 On the right side of the fabric, pin one edge of a length of the cotton tape around the basted line of one of the scooped out shapes. Baste and machine-stitch the tape in place, working close to the edge. Remove all basting stitches.

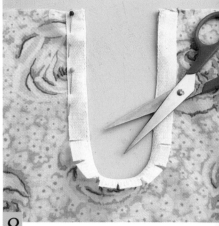

8 Turn the tape to the wrong side and press over, clipping notches around the curved edge to help it to lay flat. Pin and machine-stitch the tape in place along the outer edge, stitching over the clipped notches. Repeat steps 7 and 8 with the remaining scooped out section.

9 Press a double-fold ¾-inch hem onto the wrong side, along the top edge of the lining between the scooped shapes. Pin and machine-stitch the hem in place, stitching close to the inner edge. Press and machine-stitch a hem around the remaining lining top edge in the same manner.

10 Make the ties as shown on page 188. Thread the back tie through the shorter back top casing and between the scoops. Thread the main tie through the remaining long casing.

11 Insert the lining into the trunk, pushing it down neatly into the corners. Fold the top edges of the lining over the top of the trunk to the outside, and thread the back section under the lid between the hinges. Make sure your ties are of equal length then tie them into bows across the hinges to hold the lining in place.

here's a little more
titching to do here,
ut why not welcome
new baby by lining a
raditional wicker Moses
asket with a gathered
abric lining? The cover
gathered onto a bound
dging and ties are
ttached around the sides
hold it in place.

Covered Storage Unit

Create a great-looking cover for a plain budget-style storage unit and transform it into something special for any room in the house. This one is used in a dining room, but it would be just as practical as toy storage in a child's room or as a place to keep toiletries or linens in the bathroom.

YOU WILL NEED

- Main fabric—see below for estimating the yardage

- Lining fabric—see right for estimating the yardage

- Matching sewing thread

- Three ¾ inch diameter buttons

- A length of ⅜-inch diameter dowel to fit the width of the front flap, less ¾ inch

- Seam ripper

ESTIMATING YARDAGE

- Measure the height, width, and depth of the shelf unit.

- For the top, allow one piece of main fabric that is the width measurement by the depth measurement, plus a ⅝-inch seam allowance all around.

- For the back panel, allow one piece of main fabric that is the height measurement plus 1¾ inches for a hem and seam allowance, by the width plus 1¼ inches for seam allowances.

- For the side panels, allow two pieces of main fabric that are the height measurement plus 1¾ inches for a hem and seam allowance, by the depth measurement plus 1¼ inches for seam allowances.

- For the side-front facings, allow two main fabric strips that are the height measurement plus 1¾ inches for a hem and seam allowance, by 6 inches wide.

- For the top-front facing, allow one main fabric strip that is the width measurement by 4 inches deep.

- For the front flap, allow one piece of main fabric that is the width measurement, less 3 inches, by the height measurement, plus 3 inches for a hem and seam allowance.

- For the button-up tabs, allow for three 5 x 12½-inch strips of main fabric.

- You will need the same quantity of lining fabric as calculated for the main front flap.

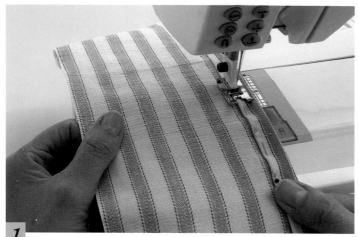

1 From the main fabric cut out one top, one back, two side panels, two side-front facings, one top-front facing, one front flap, and three tab strips. From the lining fabric, cut out one front flap. Press a ⅝-inch double-fold hem onto the wrong side along one long edge of each side-front facing. Pin and machine-stitch the hems in place.

2 With right sides together, pin the remaining long raw edge of one side-front facing to one long edge of a side panel. Machine-stitch the pieces together with a ⅝-inch seam allowance, starting the stitching ⅝-inch from the top edge. Press open the seam. Repeat the stitching with the remaining side panel and side-front facing. With right sides together, pin and machine-stitch the remaining long edges of the side panel to the back panel, as before. Press open the seams and finish edges with a machine zigzag stitch, or use a serger.

TIP

Stitch cotton tapes to the front and back side seams on the inside of the cover to tie around the frame of the storage unit and secure the cover in place.

5 Turn the cover to the right side, pin, and slipstitch the hemmed edges of the front facings to the top facing. (See page 183.)

6 Press a ⅝-inch double-fold hem to the wrong side along the bottom edge of the cover. Pin and machine-stitch in place.

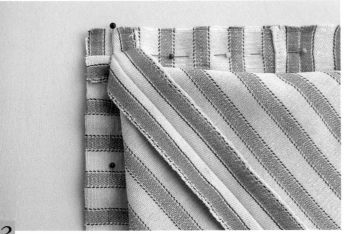

3 Lay the top panel flat with the right side up and right sides together. Pin the joined back, sides, and side-front facings to the top panel with a ⅝-inch seam allowance, matching the seams to the corners. At each corner the seam allowance should open to make a neat corner. Machine-stitch the pieces together all around the pinned edges.

4 Press a ⅝-inch double-fold hem onto the wrong side along one long edge of the top-front facing. Pin and machine-stitch the hem in place. Finish the edges with a machine zigzag stitch or use a serger. Lay the cover out flat with the right side of the top panel and wrong side of the side-front facings up. Lay the top-front facing right side down on top of the cover, with the remaining long raw edge of the facing level with the front edge of the top panel. Pin and machine-stitch the top-front facing in place with a ⅝-inch seam allowance.

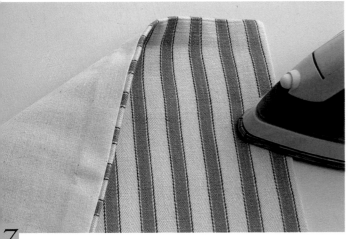

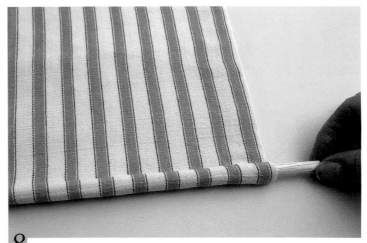

7 With right sides facing, lay the main front flap and lining piece together with raw edges matching. Pin and machine-stitch both side edges and along the top, with a ⅝-inch seam allowance. Clip the corners and turn right side out, easing out the corners with the point of a pair of scissors. Press the seamed edges flat.

8 Baste the raw bottom edges of the front flap together and press them ⅜ inch onto the wrong side, then press another ¾ inch onto the wrong side. Pin and machine-stitch the hem in place along the inner pressed edge. Insert the dowel through the hem casing and slipstitch the open ends of the hems together. (See page 183.)

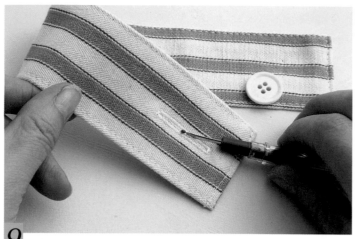

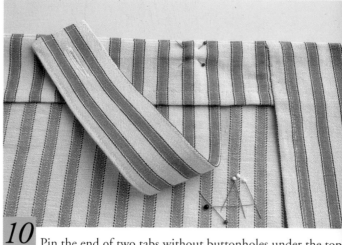

9 Make up the three tabs as shown on page 189. Stitch a 1-inch-long machine-made buttonhole at one end of each tab. Slit open the buttonholes carefully using a seam ripper.

10 Pin the end of two tabs without buttonholes under the top-front facing, placing them 1½ inches from the side-front facings. Position the remaining tab halfway between the two and pin in place.

11 Lay the front flap, lining side down, on top of the main cover, placing it centrally over the side-front facings. Align the top edge with the top of the top-front facing and cover the tabs. Pin the flap to the top-front facing. Hand-sew a button to the top of the front flap at each tab position, stitching through all layers of fabric, securing both the tabs and flap to the top-front facing. Roll up the front flap by hand, then wrap the tabs around the rolled-up front flap and fasten them to their corresponding buttons to hold in place. Slip the cover over the shelf unit and let down the front flap as required.

VARIATION

The buttoned ties on the front of the shelf cover can have multiple uses. Use the same method to make a set of wide strips and work a buttonhole in one end of each. Wrapped around a striped cotton napkin, each one makes an informal napkin ring for family suppers.

Shelf Trims

Make decorative edging for shelves from leftover fabrics and give your kitchen a country look. An iron-on interfacing allows the fabric to be cut in attractive zigzag or scalloped shapes without the risk of fraying. (See below.) Staple the trim to the top of the shelf to hold it in place. Use different fabrics for a mix-and-match feel, or trim all the shelves in the same fabric for a coordinated look.

Flounced Sink Skirt

There is no need to spend a fortune updating old bathroom fittings, especially if you love vintage style. Instead, simply dress up your existing sink with a pretty skirt and contrasting ruffle top. It looks attractive and hides unsightly plumbing.

YOU WILL NEED

- Main decorator fabric—see right for estimating yardage

- Contrast decorator fabric—see right for estimating yardage

- Matching sewing thread

- Curtain hardware—PVC-coated wires, hooks, and eyes

- Wire cutters

ESTIMATING YARDAGE

- Measure the sink from the floor to the required height and from the back wall on one side, around the front, and to the back wall on the other side.

- Allow for a piece of main fabric that is twice the width of the basin measurement, by the height, plus 1 ¼ inches for a lower hem, and ⅝ inch for a top seam allowance.

- The ruffle piece should be the same width as calculated for the main fabric, by 5 ½ inches deep.

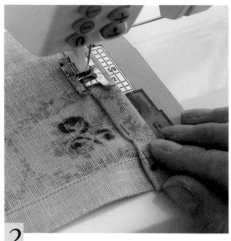

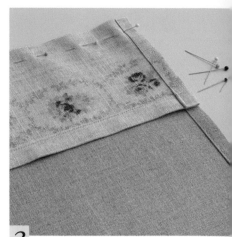

1 From the main and contrast fabrics cut out the required sink skirt pieces. Join fabric pieces, if necessary, to form the finished skirt widths. (See page 184.) On the contrast ruffle piece, press a 1-inch double-fold hem to the wrong side along one long edge. Pin and machine-stitch the hem in place.

2 Press a ⅜-inch double-fold hem onto the wrong side along the two short side edges of the contrast piece. Pin and machine-stitch the hems in place. Repeat step 2 along both side edges of the main fabric panel.

3 Lay the main fabric panel flat with the wrong side up. Place the contrast piece, wrong side up, on top of the panel, matching the top raw edges and side-hemmed edges. Pin and machine-stitch the pieces together along the top edge with a ⅝-inch seam allowance.

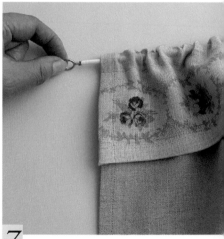

5 Measure ¾ inch down from the top edge and mark the position with a line of pins. Machine-stitch along the pinned line to form a casing along the top edge.

6 Press a ¾-inch double-fold hem onto the wrong side along the lower edge of the main panel, pin, and machine-stitch in place.

7 Install the hooks into the wall on either side of the basin at the required height. Fix a screw eye to one end of the wire and hook it onto one of the hooks. Pull the wire so that it stretches tightly around the basin and cut it to fit. Fix another eye into the cut end of the wire. Thread the wire through the casing at the top of the panel and gather it up to fit. Place the eyes over the hook, stretching the wire as before

4 Fold the attached contrast piece over onto the right side of the main panel and press the seamed edge flat.

TIPS

• Before fixing the hooks to the wall, you may need to attach small blocks of wood to ensure a stronger hold.

• If the edges of your sink basin slope down, you'll have difficulty holding the skirt in place. Use small lengths of hook-and-loop tape; stick the hook side to the front edges of the sink and hand-stitch the loop side to the wrong side of the gathered skirt top casing. Fix the skirt in place with the hooks and press the two sides of the tape together.

VARIATION

Make a simpler sink skirt by stitching a hem at the top, with two rows of machine stitching making a ruffled casing for the wire to go through.

Ironing-Board Cover

Cover your ironing board with a fabric you love. Ironing is probably not your favorite domestic chore, but somehow it will seem less of a duty and a bit of a pleasure when you're smoothing out all those creases over sumptuous vintage roses.

YOU WILL NEED

- Main decorator fabric—see right for estimating the yardage

- Matching sewing thread

- Thin cotton batting

- 3 yards of 2-inch-wide ready-made bias binding

- 4 yards of ¼-inch-wide cotton tape

- Paper for making a template

- Bodkin or safety pin

ESTIMATING YARDAGE

- Trace the shape of your ironing board onto the piece of paper and add 1⅜ inches all around. Cut the shape out to form a template.

- Allow enough fabric and batting for one 2-inch-wide template.

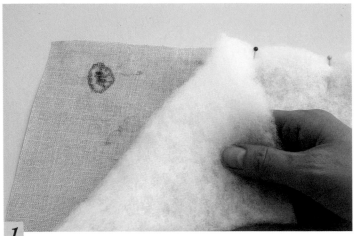

1 From both the main fabric and batting, cut out one template. Lay the main fabric piece flat, wrong side up, and place the batting on top, keeping all edges even. Pin and baste the batting to the fabric around the outer edges.

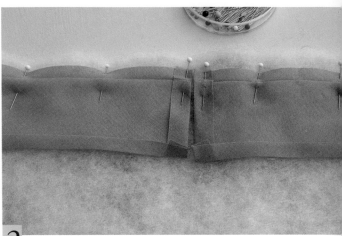

2 Open out the folds at one end of the bias binding and press ⅜ inch onto the wrong side. With the batting side of cover and the wrong side of binding facing up, pin the binding to the edges of the cover, starting at the center of the short end and opening out one long edge of the binding as you work. To finish, cut off the working end of the binding leaving ⅜ inch extra. Fold the end over to the wrong side and pin in place with the two folded ends butting together.

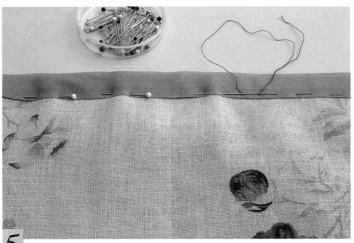

5 Pin and baste the folded edge of the binding to the right side of the cover all around the machine-stitched line.

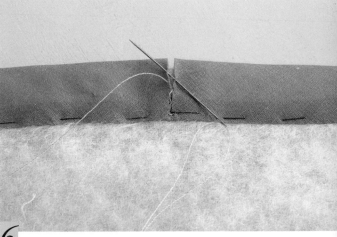

6 Working from the wrong side of the cover, oversew the ends of the binding together up to the folded edge only. (See page 183.) Machine-stitch the binding in place, then remove the basting stitches.

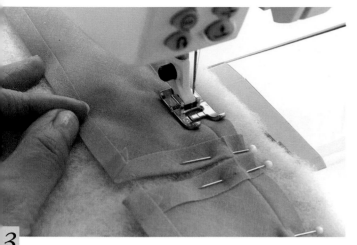

3 Machine-stitch the binding in place all around the outer edge, stitching along the opened-out binding press-line.

4 Press the binding onto the right side of the cover, aligning the binding edge with the line of machine-stitching.

7 Thread one end of the cotton tape into the bodkin or attach it to one end of the safety pin. Thread the tape through the casing and back out, leaving approximately 8 inches of tape showing at each end. Place the cover over the ironing board and pull up the tape so the cover folds underneath and fits tightly. Tie the tapes into a double bow and tuck the ends underneath the edges of the cover.

TIP

Use a hardwearing, washable linen-and-cotton blend or one hundred percent linen to make a cover that will withstand the hottest setting on your iron.

VARIATION

Even the tiniest laundry room can be neat, and a smart new cover for the ironing board will help you keep it that way.

Basic Techniques

In this section, you'll find all you need to know to make the projects featured in this book, from caring for fabrics to making a pattern, as well as all the basic stitches and sewing techniques used.

Choosing Fabrics

You can use almost any fabric for making a slipcover, from heavy tapestry to delicate cottons and lace. But when you're choosing fabrics for your projects, it is important to consider the wear and tear the final article will receive.

Obviously seat cushions and covers in busy living areas will obviously get a lot of use, so they should be made in a fabric with a firm weave. Velvet, brocade, corduroy, heavy-weight cotton, and a linen and cotton blend are all suitable. Leave chintz and cotton sateen fabrics for the bedroom or limit them to occasional chairs. Accent pillows are not as exposed to the same amount of wear, so you can use any types of fabrics, including dress materials.

Fabrics made from natural fibers, such as cotton, linen, wool, and silk, are more suitable for home furnishings, in general. Synthetics collect static electricity, and may attract more dirt.

Estimating yardage

When buying fabric, allow extra yardage if you have chosen a print and want to center a motif on each piece. It may be necessary to match patterns across seams, as well, especially on tablecloths and throws. You can run a striped fabric in different directions on box edgings and corded edgings. Or you can mix patterns and prints.

Cutting out

You will need a large flat surface and a sharp pair of scissors. Before starting, check for any fabric defects. Most stores will not exchange cloth once you have cut into it. Irregularities are often marked with a tag on the selvage—the firmly woven edge running down both sides of the fabric. On a print you may find information about the care of the fabric printed down the edges. When cutting, always trim off the selvages, and make sure that your pieces are cut straight and square (unless otherwise stated), with one side parallel to the selvage, whenever possible.

Matching pattern repeats

For a professional result, it is important that the pattern design matches across any seams. The best way to accomplish this to match pattern repeats before you begin work.

Lay one cut length of fabric, right side up on a flat surface. On another length of fabric, fold the seam allowance along one side edge and press lightly.

With right sides facing, overlap the pressed edge over the side edge of the first fabric length, matching up the pattern along the edges. Pin the pieces together, and then baste them with ladder stitch, see page 183. Remove the pins, open the seam allowances, and machine-stitch the pieces on the wrong side.

Caring for Covers and Pillows

Regular care and attention will prevent your covers from becoming too dirty.

Vacuuming

Regular vacuuming and spot-cleaning will prevent household dirt, grease, and stains from settling deep down into the fibers of your slipcovers, pillows, and cushions. Once grime has penetrated, it is often difficult to remove.

Laundering

At some point all of your slipcovers will need laundering, but tablecloths and bedcovers should be washed regularly. Make sure to choose a fabric that can take frequent washing.

Whatever cover you are making, check the fabric's care label before purchasing it. If there is no label attached to the end of the roll, ask a salesperson. If you are not sure, buy a small sample, measure it, and do a laundry test. After washing and drying, iron it. Measure it to see if it has shrunk and to check for color-fastness. If it doesn't hold up to the process, choose something else or resign yourself to dry-cleaning bills.

STITCHES

This is a selection of the most commonly used stitches for making slipcovers and pillows. In all cases, it is important to make the stitches a matching size and to keep an even tension. Use a thread that matches the color of the fabric. An exception can be made for temporary stitches, which will be easier to see in a contrasting color.

The following stitches are worked for a right-handed person; simply reverse them if you are left handed.

BASTING STITCH

This is a temporary stitch used to hold two pieces of fabric together while the permanent stitching is being done.

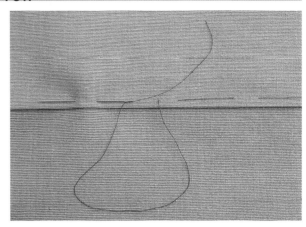

Using a contrast colored thread, work long straight stitches just inside the seam line, by moving the needle in and out of the fabric.

TAILOR'S TACKS

Tailor's tacks are used to mark construction details and matching points. These are temporary stitches, which can be time-consuming to make. Other methods of marking can be used instead, such as chalk pencils, dressmaker's carbon paper, and by making a small snip into the seam allowance.

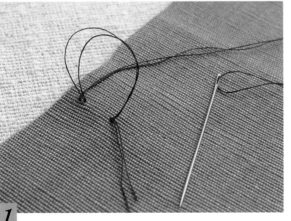

1 Using a long length of doubled thread, make a small stitch through the two layers of fabric at the position you wish to mark. Pull the needle through, leaving a long thread loop, as shown. Make a second stitch over the first one, leaving a long loop, as before.

2 Carefully fold back the top layer of fabric to the tailor's tack and pull the loops through to the inside. Using sharp scissors, cut the loops to separate the two layers of fabric.

SLIPSTITCH

This stitch is used to hold a folded hem edge to a flat surface. It is almost invisible on the right side of the fabric and is worked from right to left, holding the needle parallel to the stitching line.

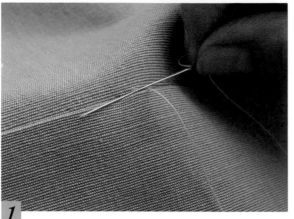

1 Secure the thread on the inside of the hem. Bring the needle out of the top fold of the hem and pick up two threads from the flat fabric directly below.

2 Insert the needle back down into the folded edge and inside the fold for approximately ⅜ inch. Bring the needle and thread back out. Continue along the hem in the same way, making sure the stitches are not pulled too tightly or the fabric will look puckered on the right side.

CATCH STITCH

Used to hold a raw edge firmly in place next to a flat surface, this stitch is worked from right to left, as in single-fold side hems, that are to be enclosed with a lining.

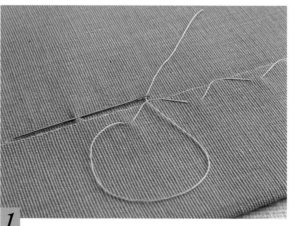

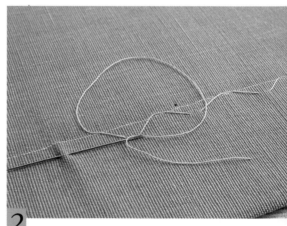

1 Secure the thread on the wrong side of the hem, then bring the needle and thread through to the right side about ⅛ inch from the raw edge. Pass the needle up and to the left, picking up two threads from the single layer of fabric.

2 Pull the needle through and pass it down to the left, taking another tiny stitch in the hem fabric. Continue along the hem in the same way.

STAY STITCH

A machine stitch made in a line to support the grain and prevent a piece of cut fabric from changing shape or dimension in the seam area.

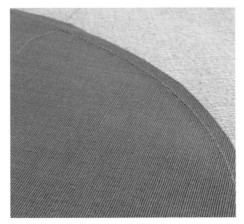

Stay stitches are made immediately after cutting out your pieces and before any handling, such as pinning and basting, which can stretch the fabric out of shape. Stay stitches are sewn into a single layer of fabric, with an even stitch length and usually about ⅜ inch from the cut edge. Stitches should be made in the direction of the grain whenever possible, to help stop distortion.

EDGE SLIPSTITCH

This is an invisible stitch that is used to join two folded edges together, as in a mitered corner.

Working from right to left, secure the thread on the wrong side, then pull the needle through one of the folded edges, then through the fold of the opposite edge for about ¼ inch. Continue working in this way, across the gap, closing the two edges.

OVERHAND STITCH

This is a tiny, even stitch, used to top-sew two finished or folded edges together, as in attaching ties, rings, or tapes.

Secure the thread on the wrong side of the fabric. Bring the needle up through the front, close to the working edge. Take the needle over the top of the edge, and pass it diagonally over to the left. Pick up one or two threads from the other edge. Pass the needle directly back through the front edge, again picking up one or two threads of the fabric. Continue in this way, keeping the stitches uniform in size and evenly spaced.

LADDER STITCH

This is a temporary stitch used to baste together seams from the right side. It is especially useful when matching patterns across seams.

Press the seam allowance to the wrong side, along one fabric piece. With right sides on top, place the pressed edge over the seam allowance of the second fabric piece, so that the pattern matches exactly across the join. Pin the fabric layers together.

Secure a needle and thread to one end of the folded edge. Bring the needle out to the right side through the fold. Take the needle horizontally across the join and straight down through the flat fabric next to the seam. Pass the needle vertically along the underside of the seam line for about ¾ inch, then bring the needle out again, through the flat fabric, close to the seam.

Take another horizontal stitch across the join back into the folded edge and run the needle along the fold for ¾ inch. Bring the needle back out again. Continue working the stitches across the join in this way, until the entire seam is closed. Fold the two fabric pieces again, right sides together, and trim the seam allowances to the same depth. Machine-stitch the pieces together along the seam line.

SEAMS

There are many types of seams, but the right one for a particular project takes into account the weight and thickness of the fabric, as well as the position of the seam. Always make sure to allow enough fabric for seam allowances, especially if the fabric is likely to fray. In that case, neatening the edges with a machine-zigzag stitch, a special serging machine, or with overhand hand stitches is recommended.

STRAIGHT STITCHED SEAM

This is perhaps the most commonly used seam used for joining fabric widths. It is best to make a ⅝-inch-wide seam allowance for slipcovers and pillows, unless otherwise stated.

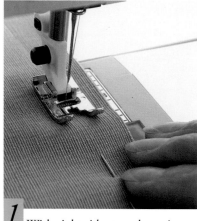

1 With right sides together, pin (and baste, if you wish) along the seam line. Machine-stitch along the seam line, making a few reverse stitches at the start and finish of the seam to secure the threads.

2 Using a steam iron, press the seam allowances open against the wrong side of the fabric.

FLAT FELL SEAM

This is another type of self-neatening seam, used mainly for heavyweight fabrics, where the raw edges are enclosed. It is stronger and flatter than a French seam.

1 With right sides together, pin the two joining edges and machine-stitch along the seam line, making a few reverse stitches at the start and finish to secure the threads. Press open the seam allowances and trim one seam allowance to ¼ inch.

2 Fold the other seam allowance in half, then fold it over to enclose the raw edge of the trimmed seam allowance. Press the seam flat.

3 Pin the seam allowances at right angles to the seam and machine-stitch them in place close to the folded edge.

FRENCH SEAM

This narrow double seam neatly contains all the raw edges. It is used mainly on unlined items, sheer and lightweight fabrics, and those that fray easily.

1 With wrong sides together, pin the two edges together and machine-stitch a line ⅜ inch from the raw edge. Trim the seam allowances to ¼ inch. Press open the seam allowances.

2 Press the seam back on itself so that the fabric is right sides together, with the seam line running along the edge. Pin and machine-stitch the seam ⅜ inch from the folded edge, enclosing the raw edges. Press the finished seam to one side.

LAPPED SEAM

Interlining and batting are made from bulky fabrics and are best joined with a lapped seam, which lays flat. Because the lapped seams will be enclosed within the item, there is no need to neaten the edges.

With both pieces of interlining right side up, overlap one raw edge directly over the other by ¾–½ inch. Pin and machine-stitch the two layers together, using either a straight or zigzag stitch. Trim away the raw edges.

REDUCING BULK

Before you turn out a seamed corner to the right side, trim away the seam allowances so that they are less bulky and sit flatter when pressed.

1 Snip the seam allowances at the corner close to the stitched line as shown. Do not cut too close, otherwise frayed edges will pop out on the finished side.

2 If the seam still appears too bulky because the fabric is thick, snip away more fabric from the seam allowance on each side of the corner in a diagonal line, as shown.

3 Use a pointed object, such as the points of a pair of scissors, to carefully push out the corner, when turning through to the right side. Do not push the pointed end through the seam.

CORDING

Cording is a soft cord covered with a narrow strip of fabric. It is sewn into a seam as a decorative edging to make the seam stronger. If your cord is not pre-shrunk, launder it at a high temperature and let it dry thoroughly before you begin. Cable cord is available in various diameters, although the medium sizes, 3 and 4, are the most commonly used.

CUTTING AND JOINING THE CORDING STRIPS

If the cording is to be used on straight edges, cut the fabric strips along the straight grain. You may also want to do this if you are using a striped fabric and want the stripes to run in a horizontal direction around the cord. However, if the cording is to curve around corners, cut the strips on the bias to help them bend (at a 45-degree angle to the horizontal and cross grains) to help them bend.

1 To find the bias of the fabric, fold down the raw edge that runs across the width of the fabric from selvage to selvage to form a triangle that lies parallel to one of the selvages. Press and cut along the fold line.

2 Draw chalk lines parallel to the bias cut line, to the required width. To gauge the strip width, measure around the cord and add the correct seam allowance (see the individual project). Alternatively, fold a corner of the fabric over the cord and pin, encasing the cord snugly. Then measure the seam allowance from the pin and cut.

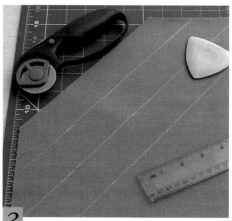

3 Open the fabric strip to find the correct cutting width. Cut along the lines using scissors or a rotary cutter, ruler, and mat, until you have the required number of strips to go around the edge of your project.

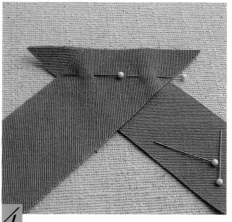

4 To join the fabric cording strips to form one long length, trim the ends at a 45-degree angle. With right sides facing, stitch the two pieces together with a ¼ inch seam allowance, as shown.

5 Press open the seam and trim the pointed ends of the seam allowances level with the edges of the strip.

JOINING CORDING ENDS

You will have to join cord ends to make one continuous seam.

Note: To enable you to see in more detail how the ends are joined, in these photos (right), the length of cording is not basted to a fabric piece.

1 Once you have basted your cording to the right side of your fabric piece, pick out about 2 inches of the cording machine stitches at each end, where the cording meets and fold back the cording fabric strips. Trim the two ends of the cable cord so that they butt together, then bind the ends with thread.

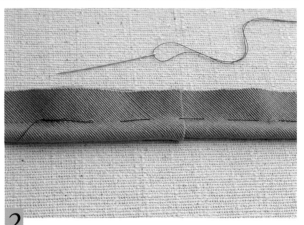

2 Turn under ⅜ inch at one end of the fabric strip to neaten, and slip it over the raw opposite end. Baste the ends together, enclosing the cable cord inside, and continue as shown in the individual project.

COVERING CABLE CORD

1 Place the cable cord on the wrong side of the cording strip and bring the long edges together, enclosing the cord. Pin the edges together.

2 Using a zipper foot on your sewing machine, stitch down the length of the cord, working as close to the cable cord as possible.

CORDING RIGHT ANGLES AND CURVES

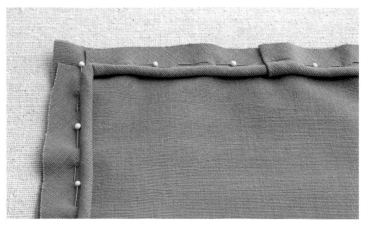

Pin and baste the cording to the right side of the one fabric piece, with raw edges level and the cord facing inward. To make the cording turn the corner, snip into the cording seam turnings close to the stitch line and bend the cord around the corner. Continue basting the cording in place as before.

If the cording is to bend gradually around a curve, snip into the cording seam turnings at several regular intervals to allow it to curve smoothly.

TIES AND TABS

There are many ways of attaching slipcovers so they stay in place. One of the most useful ways to do this is to make narrow ties that hold a chair seat, stool cover, or any other project in place. Wider ties, made from lightweight fabric, will form an elegant bow at the back of dining-chair cover, while tabs can be buttoned together to hold folded napkins or the front of a shelf cover neatly in place.

These narrow fabric ties are cut and folded like bias binding and topstitched down one edge.

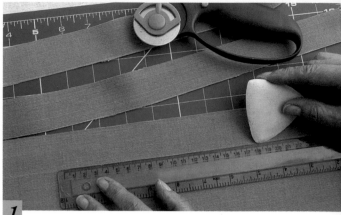

1 Draw parallel straight-grain lines across the width your fabric, to the required tie width. This should be four times the finished flat width of the ties. Cut along the lines, until you have the required length for your ties.

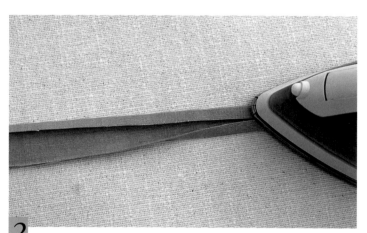

2 With wrong sides together, press the strip in half along its length. Then open the strip and press the long raw edges onto the wrong side to meet the center press line, making sure you don't burn your fingers.

3 Fold the strip in half again along its length, bringing the pressed long edges together and enclosing the raw edges completely. Pin and machine-stitch the pressed edges together along the full-length of the strip. Cut the strip into the required lengths and number of ties. Neaten the raw ends by pushing them inside the tie tubes.

MAKING FOLDED TIES

These ties are made from strips of fabric that are stitched from the wrong side and turned out so that no topstitching is visible on the right side. These ties are usually made from strips of lightweight fabric.

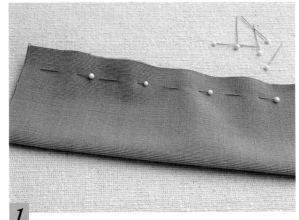

1 Cut out your tie strips to the size given in the individual project. With right sides together, fold a strip in half along its length. Pin and machine-stitch across one short end and down the long edges, with a ⅝-inch seam allowance.

2 Clip the corners and trim the seam allowances then turn the tie out to the right side. Press flat with the seams running long the edges. If your project requires neat ends, fold the seam allowance to the inside at the open end, and slipstitch the edges together. (See page 183.)

MAKING TABS

These are made in a similar way to the narrow ties, in which the seam allowances are pressed to the wrong side and the tab is then topstitched together.

1 Press a ⅜-inch seam allowance onto the wrong side along the two long edges of the tab strip and across one short end.

2 With wrong sides facing, fold the tab in half along its length bringing the long pressed edges together. Press the folded tab flat and pin the fabric layers together around all sides.

3 Topstitch the tab together, working close to the edge and sewing up one long side, across the neatened short end, and back down the other long side, removing the pins as you work. Press the tab flat.

PLEATS

Pleats are folds in the fabric formed by folding a continuous length of fabric onto itself. The exception is a pleat with a separate underlay, or backing piece, stitched to the back. Pleats will hang best if they are folded along the straight grain of the fabric and pressed in place. Basically, pleats are folded along a specific fold line, and the fold is aligned with another line, the placement line.

FORMING INVERTED PLEATS

Inverted pleats have two fold lines and a common placement line. In other words, the pleat edges butt together, with each pleat folding away from the other.

1 Mark the center position of the placement line along the top and lower edges of your fabric piece with hand-sewn tailor's tacks. (See page 181.)

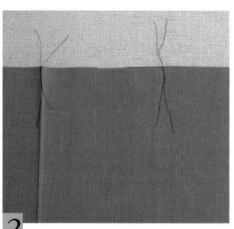

2 Measure the finished depth of each pleat, along the top and lower edges of the fabric piece and each side of the placement line, and mark the pleat fold-line positions with tailor's tacks. (See the individual project.) With wrong sides facing, fold the fabric along each fold-line position and press folds in place.

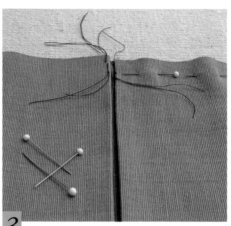

3 Working from the right side of the fabric, fold along one of the pressed fold-lines and, matching the tailor's tacks, bring the pressed edge over to align with the center placement line. Pin in place. Repeat with the second side of the pleat.

4 Baste the pleats in place along the top and lower edges.

MITERS

Two simple-fold hems can be folded into a miter to make a flat, neat corner. As the hems have raw edges, neaten them with a machine zigzag or use a serger.

A miter is used to form a neat, flat finish to a corner where two hems meet.

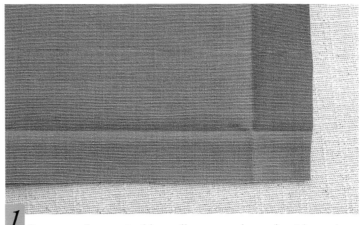

1 Press over the required hem allowances, down the side, and along the lower edges, and open it flat again.

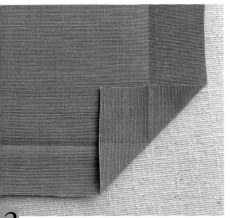

2 Matching up the press lines, turn over the corner of the fabric so that the diagonal fold passes through the point where the two press lines cross.

3 Press the diagonal fold in place, and then trim away the pointed corner, leaving a ⅝-inch seam allowance.

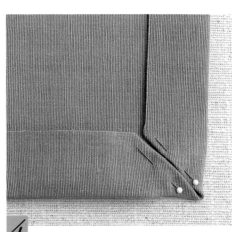

4 Fold the side and lower hems back in place and pin the diagonal mitered edges. The hem is now ready to be stitched in place.

MAKING A PATTERN FOR AN ARMCHAIR

A slipcover pattern for an armchair is cut and pinned together on the chair itself to ensure a good fit. Make your pattern using a cheap cotton fabric, such as muslin, and remember to remove any box seat cushions from the chair before you begin. The same method can be used for making a pattern for a sofa. To cover the seat cushions follow the instructions given for the "Box-Edged Bench Cushions" on page 94.

YOU WILL NEED

- Muslin—see right for estimating the yardage
- Sharp scissors
- Dressmaking pins
- Pencil
- Paper for making the finished patterns

TIP

After you have cut out the pattern pieces, write the names of the pieces on the patterns, marking the top and bottom edges, fold positions, and how many of each piece you will need.

ESTIMATING YARDAGE

- There is no need to make a muslin pattern for the whole chair; a half pattern is sufficient. Mark the halfway position of the chair with a row of pins from the front bottom edge, over the seat, up the inner back and down the outer back to the bottom edge. You can then use the pattern to cut out your pieces from double-thickness fabric, placing the outer back, inner back, seat, and front box-edging pieces to a fold of fabric.

- For the front and back: measure from the bottom of the chair up the outer back; over the top edge, down the inner back, across the seat, and down to the front base edge of the chair (A on diagram, opposite). Measure across half the width of the back at the widest point (B on the diagram). Add 2 inches to the width for the side seams and 10 inches to the length for a tuck-in allowance.

- For the outside arm pieces: measure from the bottom of the chair, up the outside of the arm, to where the arm starts to curve and mark where you have measured up to with pins (C on the diagram). Measure the length of the outside arm at the longest point (D on the diagram). Add 4 inches to the depth measurement for a base hem and top seam allowance, plus 2 inches to the length measurement for side seam allowances.

- For the inside arm pieces: measure from the base of the curve on the outside arm (from the pin positions), over the top of the arm, to the seat on the inside (E on the diagram). Measure the length of the inner arm along the top edge (F on the diagram). Add 5 inches to the depth measurement for a tuck-in allowance and a top seam allowance, plus 2 inches to the length measurement for side seam allowances.

- For the front arm: measure from the base of the chair to the top of the arm (G on the diagram). Measure the width of the arm at the widest point (H on the diagram). Add 2 inches to the width measurement for seam allowances and 4 inches to the depth for a hem.

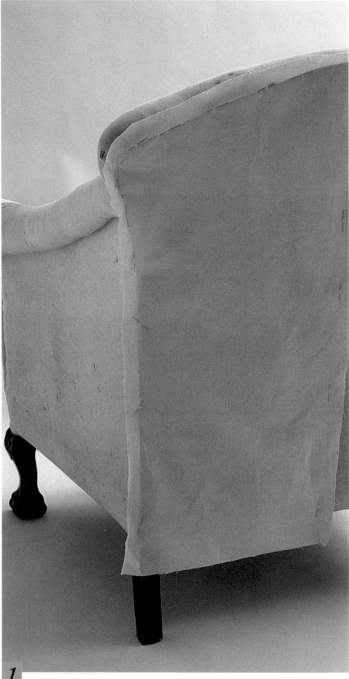

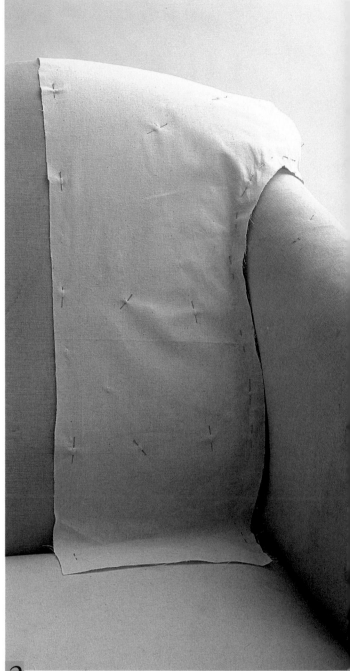

1 Align the straight edge of a piece of muslin with the pin line on the outer back of the chair, and temporarily pin the piece to the chair. Cut around the shape of the back, leaving a 2-inch seam allowance around the top and side edges and a 4-inch overhang at the bottom.

2 Cut another piece of muslin for the inner front adding 4 inches to the length for the tuck-in at the bottom and plenty of fabric to go over the top of the chair to the outer back. Lay the fabric over the chair, with the top draping over the back and the tuck-in allowance lying on the seat. Align one straight edge with the chair's center pin-line and temporarily pin the piece in place. Trim the fabric around the arm shape, leaving a 1-inch seam allowance around the arm shaping.

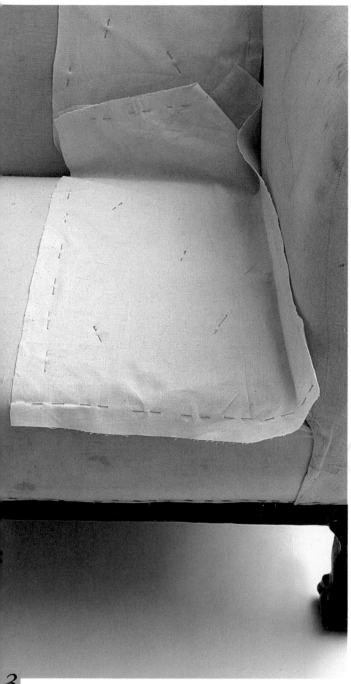

3 Cut a piece of muslin for the seat, adding 4 inches for the tuck-in allowance to both the length and width measurements, and 1 inch to the length for a front seam allowance. Pin the seat section to the chair, aligning one straight edge with the center pin line and letting the tuck-in sections lay against the inner back and inside arm.

4 Cut a front box-edging piece to fit half the front of the chair seat, adding 4 inches to the depth measurement and 1 inch to the width for a seam allowance. Pin the piece to the seat front edge, aligning one short end with the center pin line.

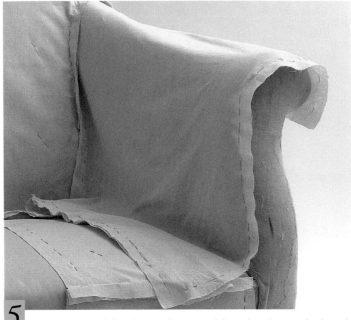

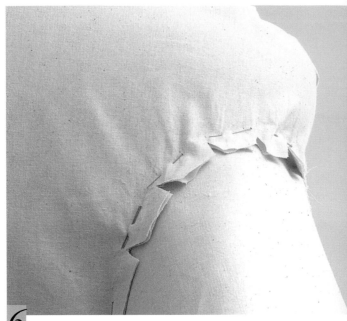

5 Cut out a panel for the inside arm, adding 4 inches to the length for a tuck-in. Place the panel over the arm, aligning the top edge with the pin line at the bottom of the arm curve (on the outside arm), with a 1-inch seam allowance. Lay the tuck-in allowance on the seat. Trim the back edge of the inside arm panel to fit the arm shape. Pin the inside arm to the inner back along the back edge.

6 Snip into the seam allowances around the top edge of the arm to create a smooth curve, easing in the inner back panel to fit as you go.

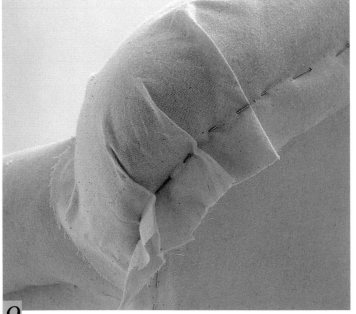

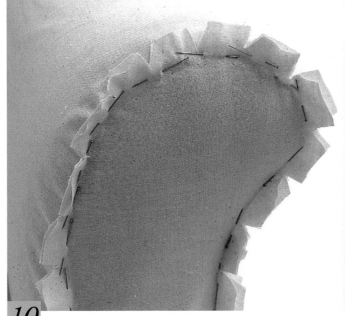

9 If the top edges of the chair back curve like the one shown, pin pleats around the top edge of the inner front piece to fit it to the back piece. Trim away excess fabric from the top edge of the inner front, leaving a 1-inch seam allowance. Pin the inner and outer back pieces together along the top edge, as shown.

10 Snip into the seam allowances around the curved edges of the arm.

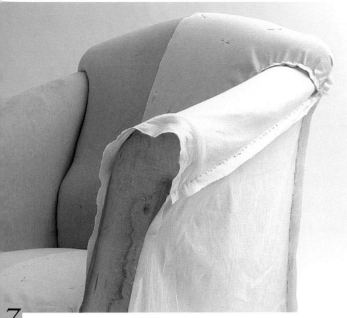

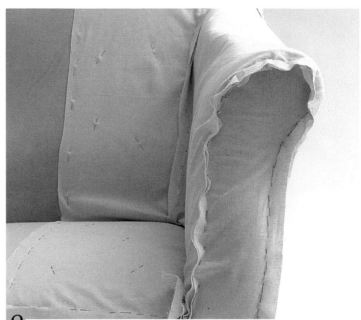

7 Cut out a panel for the outside arm, adding 4 inches to the depth for a hem allowance and 2 inches to the width for seam allowances. Pin the outside arm piece to the outer back panel along the back edge and the top edge to the top of the inside arm piece.

8 Cut out a front arm piece and add 4 inches to the length for a hem allowance and 2 inches to the width for seam allowances. Pin the piece to the front arm, along the inside and outside arm pieces, trimming the fabric to fit around the curved top edge and leaving a 1-inch seam allowance all around.

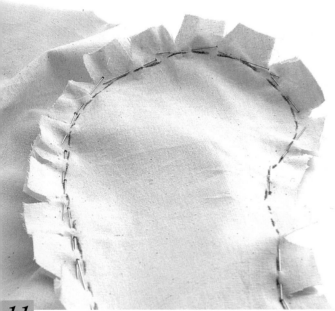

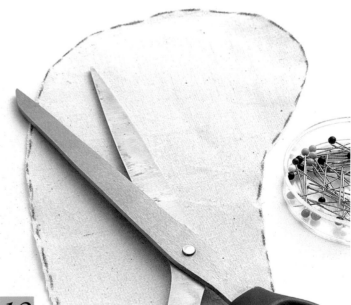

11 Adjust the pinning all around the muslin pattern, so that it fits neatly. Then, carefully draw around all the pinned seams using a pencil, along the bottom edges of the chair and mark the positions of any pleats. Remove the muslin pattern from the chair.

12 Unpin the pattern pieces and trim away the seam allowances following the pencil lines. Press the pattern pieces flat. Trace the muslin pieces onto the paper, smoothing off the lines, and add a ¾-inch seam allowance to all edges.

MAKING A PATTERN FOR A DINING CHAIR

Make a pattern from plain muslin to fit the seat of an upholstered dining chair, before cutting out your main decorator fabric. Using a muslin template will also help you to position any large patterns in the right place. Folding in darts at the front edge will ensure that you get a neat fit and a professional-looking slipcover.

YOU WILL NEED

- Muslin—see below for estimating yardage
- Sharp scissors
- Dressmaking pins
- Pencil
- Paper for making the finished patterns

ESTIMATING YARDAGE

- There is no need to make a muslin pattern for the whole chair seat; a half pattern is sufficient. Mark the halfway position of the chair seat with a row of pins from the front bottom edge, over the seat to the back bottom edge. The pattern is then used with double-thickness fabric, placing the seat and skirt pieces to the fold of the fabric.

- Measure the seat from the bottom of the front edge to the bottom edge of the back (A on the diagram, right), and add 6 inches extra to the length at the back.

- Measure the seat from the center pin line to the bottom of the seat at the side (B on the diagram).

- Measure for the skirt piece from the center pinned line around the side of the chair to the center back (C on the diagram), and add 1 inch to the length for a seam allowance.

- For the skirt depth, allow about 6 inches.

MAKING THE PATTERN

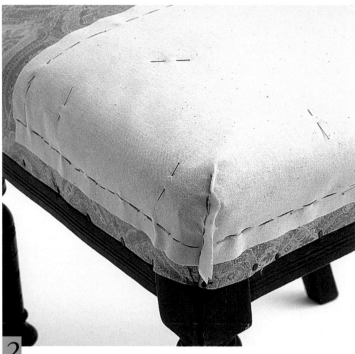

1 Lay a piece of muslin over the seat, aligning one long edge with the center pin line and letting the extra fabric hang down at the back. Pin the muslin to the front and side edges of the pad, leaving a ⅝-inch seam allowance all around.

2 Pin a dart in the muslin at the front edge of the seat to fit the fabric around the corner. Pin a line about 2 inches down from the padded edge of the chair, from the center-pinned front to the back legs, to mark the stitch line of the skirt.

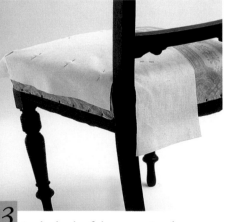

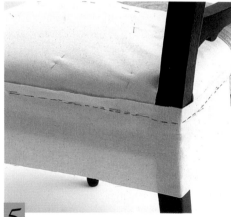

3 At the back of the seat, trim the muslin around the wooden frame, leaving a ⅝-inch seam allowance around all edges.

4 Pin a skirt piece of the required depth all around the seat piece from the pinned center front, pinning on top of the previous pinned line, using a ⅝-inch seam allowance. Take the skirt piece around the legs to finish at the center back.

5 Check that you are happy with the fit of the muslin pattern, adjusting pins if necessary. Then draw around the pinned seam lines and the dart position, using a pencil. Unpin the muslin pieces and trim away the seam allowances following the pencil lines. Press the pattern pieces flat. Trace around the muslin pieces onto the paper, smoothing the lines and adding a ⅝-inch seam allowance to all edges.

MAKING A HEADBOARD

These are basic instructions for making a padded headboard, which can be covered in a decorative fabric to coordinate with the bed linen or soft furnishings, as in the project illustrated on page 136.

TIP

If you are not able to attach the headboard to the bed, increase the depth of the medium-density fiberboard board to about 54 inches (from the floor to your chosen height) and cover just the top section of the board, i.e. from the top of the mattress to the top of the headboard. To neaten the lower edges of the fabric, simply fold the raw edges under and staple them to the board. The board can sit on the floor behind the bed. When the bed is pushed firmly against the wall, it will hold the headboard in place.

YOU WILL NEED

- ¾-inch thick medium density fiberboard (MDF) or plywood that is approximately 30 inches high (measuring from the top of the bed base to your chosen height), by the width of the bed. (Join lengths of board if necessary using metal T-brackets, to obtain the correct width.)
- Lightweight batting—see below for estimating the yardage
- Muslin—see below for estimating the yardage
- Staple gun
- Two 35-inch pieces of 2 x 1 inch wood (such as pine) with a vertical ⅜-inch wide slot cut up the center of each piece to fit over the headboard fixing bolts on the end of your bed (the length of the slots will depend on the height of your bolts). Note: if your bed does not have fixing bolts, refer to the tip, below left.
- 1¼-inch-long wood screws

ESTIMATING YARDAGE

- Allow for a piece of batting that measures the same as the board, plus 2 inches around all sides for a wrap-around allowance. You may need to join batting widths to obtain the correct size for your headboard. If so, join pieces with lapped seams. (See page 185.)
- The muslin front piece needs to be the same size as the batting. Join fabric widths, if necessary, to obtain the correct size.
- The muslin backing piece needs to be the finished size of the board. Join fabric widths, if necessary, to obtain the correct size.

MAKING UP

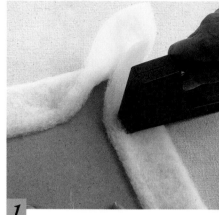

1 Cut out the fabric pieces from muslin and batting as described. Lay the batting flat and place the board in the center, so that 2 inches of the batting shows around all edges. Fold the batting over onto the back of the board and staple it in place. The staples should be approximately 2 inches apart.

5 Make a diagonal cut across one corner to trim away a triangular section of excess fabric. Fold under the remaining raw edges of the corner fabric to form a neat miter. Repeat at the remaining corners.

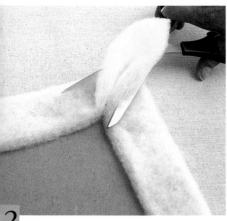

2 Using scissors, make a diagonal cut in the batting at each corner to trim excess.

3 Staple the batting in place at the trimmed corners, placing the staples at right angles to the diagonal join.

4 Lay the muslin front piece flat and place the board on top, in the center, with the padded side down and 2 inches of fabric showing all around the edges. Staple the muslin to the board as shown in step 1, but gently pull the muslin as you work to obtain a smooth fit.

6 Staple across the mitered corners to hold the fabric in place.

7 Press a ¾-inch single-fold hem onto the wrong side along all sides of the muslin backing piece.

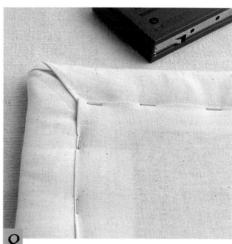

8 Lay the padded board face down on a flat surface. Place the backing piece on top, in the center, wrong sides up. Staple the backing piece in place around the pressed edges at roughly 2-inch intervals. Drill and screw the timber pieces securely to the back of the padded board, in line with the bolts. Attach the board to the bed using the bolts.

ZIPPERS

Zippers are used in many of the slipcover projects to form a neat, unobtrusive opening. Insert the zipper between two seams before you begin to assemble the cover. The zipper is usually 3 or 4 inches shorter than the finished width of the pillow form or back boxing strip.

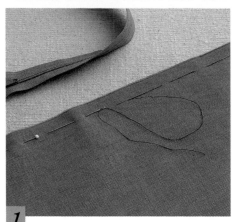

1 With right sides facing, pin and baste the two edges of the seam in which the zipper is to be inserted.

2 Lightly press open the seam. Lay the zipper over the seam, in the center, and mark the two ends of the zipper with pins.

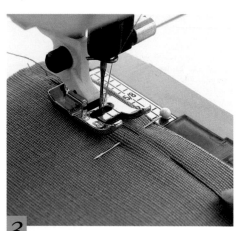

3 Remove the zipper, and with right sides of fabric facing, machine-stitch the seam at each end, from the side edges to the pin markers. Reverse-stitch at each end to secure. Press open the seam.

4 Lay the zipper face down onto the seam allowances, along the basted section of the seam. Make sure the zipper teeth are exactly over the seam line, then baste the zipper in place.

5 Working from the right side and using a zipper foot on your machine, carefully sew the zipper in place. Stitch a ¼ inch from each side of the seamline and across the top and bottom of the zipper in one single line. Unpick all of the basting stitches and check to see that the zipper opens easily.

Resources

Fabric used in the projects

Pages 22–27 Dining-Chair Cover
Main fabric: The Seasons, Red, GP and Baker.

Pages 28–31 Ruffle-Edged Chair Pad
Stripe and Dash Linen Union Cranberry, Vanessa Arbuthnott. Variation: page 30, Vanessa Arbuthnott.

Pages 34–39 Slipper-Chair Cover
Acorn and Leaf Linen Union, Straw, Vanessa Arbuthnott. Variations: page 39, both Elanbach.

Pages 40–45 Tied Dining-Chair Cover
Shot Cotton, Tangerine, Rowan. Variation: page 45, Cath Kidston.

Pages 46–53 Tailored Armchair Cover
Antique French linen. Step-by-step fabric: Pasha, Rice, Malabar. Bowls and vases: Breez. Throw: Sandra Jane. Radiator cover: Ali. Variations: page 52, left Biggie Best, right Vanessa Arbuthnott; page 53, Vanessa Arbuthnott.

Pages 54–57 Arm Cover
Posy, Pink, Elanbach.

Pages 60–63 Bound-Edged Throw
Main fabric: Solano, Cadmium; contrast fabric: Indian Organza, Gold Book, Malabar. Variation: page 63, Laura Ashley.

Pages 66–69 Garden-Chair Pad and Glider-Cover
Andrei, Green, Elanbach. Variation: page 69, Vanessa Arbuthnott.

Pages 70–73 Box-Edged Stool Cover
Patry, 03, Malabar. Variation: page 73, Sail Broad Stripe, Green, Jane Churchill.

Pages 76–77 Lace-Up Seat Cover
Deckchair canvas: John Lewis. Grommet kit: Coats Crafts UK.

Pages 78–81 The Easiest Pillow
Hatley, Cerise, Cabbages and Roses. Variation: page 81, top Biggie Best.

Pages 82–85 Monogrammed Pillow
Antique French linen. Variations: page 85, top Rowan, lower Biggie Best.

Pages 86–89 Tailored Square Pillow
Main fabric: Ambika 05; contrast backing fabric: Jellabee 02; cording fabric: Lodi 01, Malabar. Variation: page 89, Kate Forman.

Pages 90–93 Flanged Pillow
Canara, 06, Malabar.

Pages 94–99 Box-Edged Bench Cushions
Feather and Egg, Raspberry, Vanessa Arbuthnott. Variations: page 98, Rowan; page 99, Elanbach.

Pages 99–103 Shaped Box-Edged Cushion
Main fabric: Isla, 12; cable cord fabric: Tulsa, 01, Malabar. Foam: Pentonville Rubber. Variation: page 103, bench cushion, Malabar; floral cushions: Cath Kidston.

Pages 104–105 Tied Stool Cover
Roman Glass, GP 01-PK, Rowan.

Pages 106–109 Tied Neckroll Pillow
Main fabric: Dotty, Lettuce; lining fabric: Polka Dot Check, Lettuce and lavender, Vanessa Arbuthnott.

Pages 110–113 Tailored Bolster Pillow
Main fabric: Canara, 03; end contrast fabric: Talinga 04; cable cord fabric: Tulsa, 01, Malabar. Variation: page 113, Vanessa Arbuthnott.

Pages 114–119 Beanbag Chair
Main fabric: Minto Silk Stripe, 01; contrast fabric: Shamois, 20, Malabar. Polystyrene beanbag filling: Pentonville Rubber. Variations: page 118, Jane Churchill; page 119, Rowan.

Pages 122–125 Duvet Cover
Main fabric: Seaweed and Shells cotton, Cranberry/Rose pink; backing fabric: Denim/Forget-me-not, Vanessa Arbuthnott. Variation: page 125 Laura Ashley.

Pages 126–129 Self-Bordered Sham Cover
Seaweed and Shells cotton, Denim/Forget-me-not, Vanessa Arbuthnott. Variation: page 129, Laura Ashley.

Pages 130–135 Pleated Dust Ruffle
Starfish and Coral Cotton, Seapink/Rose
Pink/Cranberry, Vanessa Arbuthnott.
Variation: page 135, Coloroll.

Pages 136–139 Headboard Cover
Dimity, 17, Malabar.

Pages 140–143 Bedroom Stool Cover
Lichen, White, Elanbach. Variation:
page 143, Cath Kidston.

Pages 146–149 Circular Tablecloth
Summer Garden Check, Green, Elanbach.

Pages 150–153 Weighted Tablecloth
Broad Check, 01, Rowan.

Pages 154–157 Ruched Lampshade
Sprig, Kate Forman.

Pages 158–163 Lined Wicker Trunk
Forget-me-not rose, GP 08-C, Rowan.
Variations: page 162, basket on wheels,
Sandra Jane; page 163, Rowan.

Pages 164–169 Covered Storage Unit
Tulsi, 17, Malabar. Variation: page 168,
Laura Ashley.

Pages 172–175 Flounced Sink Skirt
Main fabric: plain linen; contrast fabric:
Cameo Rose, both Kate Forman. Variation:
page 175, Vanessa Arbuthnott.

Pages 176–179 Ironing-Board Cover
Roses, Kate Forman. Variation: page 179,
Cath Kidston.

Other sources

US

A.C. Moore
866-342-8802
www.acmoore.com

Laura Ashley
www.lauraashley-usa.com

Calico Corners
1-800-213-6366
www.calicocorners.com

Cath Kidston
+44 (0)1480 431 415
www.cathkidston.com

Coats and Clark
(800) 648-1479
www.coatsandclark.com

Cowtan & Tout
Distributors of Jane
Churchill, Manuel Canovas
and Colefax & Fowler
(212) 647-6900
www.cowtan.com

Craft Site Directory
Useful online resource
www.craftsitedirectory.com

Crafts etc.
1-800-888-0321
www.craftsetc.com

Emma One Sock
215-542-1082
www.emmaonesock.com

Hancock Fabrics
877-322-7427
www.hancockfabrics.com

Hobby Lobby
Stores throughout the US
www.hobbylobby.com

Husqvarna Viking
800-358-0001
www.husqvarnaviking.com

Jo-ann Fabric & Crafts
1-888-739-4120
www.joann.com

Michaels
1-800-642-4235
www.michaels.com

Rowan USA
+44 (0)1484 681881
www.knitrowan.com

Canada

B.B. Bargoons
1-800-665-9227
www.bbbargoons.com

Fabricland/Fabricville
Over 170 stores in Canada
www.fabricland.com
www.fabricville.com

InVU Drapery
905-828-2022
www.invudraperyco.com

Timmel Fabrics
1-877-825-9048
www.timmelfabrics.com

Wazoodle
1-866-473-4628
www.wazoodle.com

Photographic credits
Page 12: Laura Ashley
Page 13: top and bottom, Biggie Best
Page 14: left and right, Biggie Best
Page 15: Biggie Best
Page 16: Biggie Best
Page 17: top left, Wilman; top right, Biggie Best; bottom, Biggie Best
Page 18: Biggie Best
Page 19: Biggie Best

Index

Page numbers in bold refer to photographs